DUMBARTON OAKS
MEDIEVAL LIBRARY

Jan M. Ziolkowski, General Editor

THE OLD ENGLISH POEMS

OF CYNEWULF

DOML 23

The Old English Poems of Cynewulf

Edited and Translated by

ROBERT E. BJORK

DUMBARTON OAKS
MEDIEVAL LIBRARY

HARVARD UNIVERSITY PRESS
CAMBRIDGE, MASSACHUSETTS
LONDON, ENGLAND
2013

Library of Congress Cataloging-in-Publication Data
Cynewulf.
    The Old English poems of Cynewulf / edited and translated by
    Robert E. Bjork.
        pages cm. — (Dumbarton Oaks medieval library ; DOML 23)
    Includes bibliographical references and index.
    Old English text on the verso; English translation on the recto.
    ISBN 978-0-674-07263-3 (alk. paper)
    1. Christian poetry, English (Old) — Translations into English. I. Bjork,
    Robert E., 1949– II. Cynewulf. Poems. III. Cynewulf. Poems. English.
    IV. Title.
PR1642.B56 2013
829K.4 — dc23   2012037857

Contents

Introduction

Named Anglo-Saxon poets are rare, especially those who composed in the vernacular.[1] The Venerable Bede, who wrote his *Historia ecclesiastica* (*Ecclesiastical History of the English People*) ca. 731, is one, but only a single five-line Old English poem — his "Death Song" — is uncompellingly attributed to him.[2] Cædmon, the illiterate herdsman whom Bede describes in the *Ecclesiastical History* as miraculously and spontaneously producing Christian poetry in traditional Old English verse form at the injunction of an angel visiting him in the stable, is a second. Readers have known of him ever since. As "an Englishman who was suddenly made a poet by divine Providence,"[3] he even earned John Milton's empathetic admiration in his *Commonplace Book*. But a third and one of the most important named vernacular poets of the Anglo-Saxons went unrecognized until the middle of the nineteenth century. N. S. F. Grundtvig, the prolific and influential Danish scholar, poet, and theologian, made the first modern transcription of the Exeter Book in 1830 and 1831, but he did not know what to make of the passages with runes in two of the poems.[4] When in 1840 the Cambridge scholar John Kemble discovered that the runic letters actually spelled out a person's name — Cynewulf — he excitedly attributed all the poetry in the Exeter and Vercelli anthologies of Old English poetry to him. Other enthusiasts went considerably further, averring that whatever Old English poem Cædmon had not written, Cynewulf had.[5]

Yet we still do not know who Cynewulf was despite attempts to give the name a local habitation. Northumbria is one possibility, and Cynewulf, bishop of Lindisfarne (d. ca. 783), has been considered a reasonable candidate within that region. East Anglia is also possible, with Cynulf, a priest of Dunwich (fl. 803), being a likely candidate. Wessex, too, has been mentioned because of the presence there of Cynewulf, the father of Bishop Cyneweard of Wells (d. ca. 975) and a potential poet, but if the poems were written in an Anglian dialect, as is likely, then a poet writing in Wessex is more difficult to explain.[6] Peterborough has also been regarded as a possible home for the poet, because of the Abbot Cenwulf or Kenulf (d. 1006) of the monastery there.[7] But the name Cynewulf was a fairly common one, so our poet could have lived elsewhere in England and been one of a large number of clergymen bearing that name and having sufficient talent to compose poetry.[8]

The presence of the name "Cynwulf" or "Cynewulf" in runic letters (ᚳᚣᚾᚹᚢᛚᚠ = Cynwulf; ᚳᚣᚾᛖᚹᚢᛚᚠ = Cynewulf) at the end of two poems, two in the Exeter Book (*Christ II* and *Juliana*) and two in the Vercelli Book (*The Fates of the Apostles* and *Elene*), then, leads us nowhere in trying to identify the person behind the runes. One recent scholar has even argued that Cynewulf is a modern myth, not a medieval reality, so there is no person to be found at all.[9] Still others have pointed out the anachronism involved in considering Cynewulf an author in the modern sense, that is, as the sole creator of an individual work of art. He worked within a tradition that was accretive and collaborative in nature and may have merely attached his name to poems that had already been composed.[10] And the runic signature itself—the runic alphabet, or futhark, was created by the Germanic peoples some time after the birth of Christ[11]—compounds the perplexities. Why, first of all, does the signature appear in those four poems, and why in runes? Some speculate that Cynewulf's signing his work fits in with the ancient Germanic practice of signing art objects with runes;[12] some see it as participating in a vogue among contemporary Latin writers for using acrostics;[13] some regard it as signaling the shift from orality to literacy;[14] some think it is a simple request for the reader's prayers;[15] and at least one scholar thinks that it may reveal a change in attitude about the role of the author in Old English verse.[16]

A second perplexity about the runic signature is how it works. Runic letters have the virtue and the defect of being multivalent. They can stand for letters alone, and therefore the sequence of runes ᚳ-ᚣ-ᚾ-ᛖ-ᚹ-ᚢ-ᛚ-ᚠ simply spells out the name CYNEWULF. Or they can signify objects beyond themselves. Thus ᚳ means both the letter *c* and the word *cen* ("torch"); ᚣ, the letter *y* and the word *yr* ("bow," "yew," "sharp instrument," or "horn"); ᚾ, the letter *n* and the word *nied* ("need," "constraint," or "hardship"); ᛖ, the letter *e* and the word *eoh* ("horse" or "steed"); ᚹ, the letter *w* and the word *wynn* ("joy"); ᚢ, the letter *u* and the word *ur* ("aurochs" or "our"); ᛚ, the letter *l* and the word *lagu* ("water"); and ᚠ, the letter *f* and the word *feoh* ("wealth"). Cynewulf seems to use both senses of the runes, the alphabetic and the lexical, simultaneously in his poems, but there is no consensus on the precise interpretation of the signature in any one poem.[17] In the translations that follow, therefore, I leave each runic letter in place and offer a literal rendition of the surrounding text. Further explanations are found in the Notes to the Translations, which the reader can use to decide just how to decode what Cynewulf meant to convey each time he signed his name. Such decoding on the part of the reader seems to be what the poet wanted.

The puzzle of Cynewulf, then, remains unsolved, and identifying him lies beyond our abilities at the moment and may forever do so. So may locating him temporally, although there is general agreement on his earliest and latest possible dates, which are 750 and ca. the late tenth century. The earlier date is deduced from the spelling of Cynewulf's name. Evidence from coins and charters indicates that the name was spelled "Cyniwulf" before the middle of the eighth century south of the Humber and before the middle of the ninth century north of the Humber. The spelling changed to "Cynewulf" thereafter in both areas. If Cynewulf was a Mercian, therefore, he likely wrote after ca. 750 and if a Northumbrian, after ca. 850.[18] The second or latest possible date is simply that of the time when the Exeter Book and the Vercelli Book were compiled, some time in the second half of the tenth century.[19] Cynewulf lived, therefore, between the mid-eighth and late tenth centuries. We cannot, at present, be much more precise, beyond saying that the language of Cynewulf's works is not as seemingly archaic as that of some other works, such as *Beowulf,* nor as innovative as that of works of the late tenth century, such as *The Battle of Maldon.*

Ignorant though we may be about where and when Cynewulf wrote, we are fairly confident now in the twenty-first century that he did not write all twelve poems once assigned to him in the late nineteenth: these include his four signed poems as well as *Guthlac A, Guthlac B, Christ I, Christ III, Physiologus* (or *The Panther, The Whale,* and *The Partridge*), *The Phoenix, Andreas,* and *The Dream of the Rood.* Because of the work of S. K. Das, Claes Schaar, and Robert E. Diamond in the 1940s and 1950s on the style and diction of Cynewulf, most scholars consider only the four signed poems to be his. For metrical, stylistic, and thematic reasons, some maintain that *Guthlac B,* the ending of which is lost and conceivably a runic signature along with it, may also be Cynewulf's composition.[20] The arguments are persuasive, and I share that point of view, so the poem is included in this volume as one of his five poems. Like just about everything else concerning Cynewulf, the order in which he composed his poems remains unknown, but some scholars feel that he wrote *Elene* last because of the maturity and sophistication it possesses. *Guthlac B* displays a comparable maturity and sophistication.[21] The poems are presented in this volume, however, in the order in which they appear in the Exeter Book and the Vercelli Book, not in a hypothesized chronological order of composition.

FROM THE EXETER BOOK: *CHRIST II* OR *THE ASCENSION*

What may be his best composition (but see *Elene*), *Christ II* is Cynewulf's profound meditation on the reality and meaning of Christ's ascension after his death and resurrection. It unites the two other poems in the Exeter Book about Christ, *Christ I* (concerning the Advent), and *Christ III* (concerning the Last Judgment).[22] It made such a tremendous impression on N. S. F. Grundtvig when he transcribed the Exeter Book in 1830 and 1831 that he based two hymns on the poem; one of those hymns is still sung in Danish churches on Ascension Day.[23] The poem's primary source is the final three sections of Gregory the Great's 29th homily on the gospels, in which Gregory poses the simple question of why angels wore white robes at the ascension but not at the incarnation.[24] The answer, which Cynewulf offers indirectly, is that Christ, angels, and mortals were all exalted at the ascension because Christ had completed his mission of saving humankind from sin but were humbled at the incarnation when that mission began. We should be grateful for all God's gifts, the greatest of which is salvation offered us through the ascension, which Cynewulf describes as a jump or leap: "It will become known that the King of angels, the Creator strong in his powers, will jump upon the mountain, leap upon the high downs, envelop hills and knolls with his glory, redeem the world, all earth-dwellers, through that noble jump" (ll. 715–19). And he then proceeds to articulate the minor leaps that lead to the all-important one: first the incarnation, then the nativity, then the crucifixion, then the burial, then the descent into hell, and finally, the ascension. Cynewulf admonishes his audience to be ready for the Last Judgment and concludes his rumination with an extended simile reminiscent of that found in *The Seafarer,* in which the life of mortals is likened to a sea voyage:

Now it is just as if we sail in ships on the sea-flood over cold water throughout the broad sea, in sea-steeds, travel in wood-floaters. That stream is dangerous, the waves without end that we toss on here throughout this mutable world, windy the billows over the deep water-way. The plight was hard before we had sailed to land over the rough ocean-ridge. Then help came to us, that led us to salvation in the harbor, the spiritual son of God, and gave us the gift that we might know over the ship's side where we must moor our sea-steeds, the old wave-mares, fast with anchors. Let us fix our hope in that harbor, which for us the ruler of the skies, holy in the heights, opened when he ascended to heaven. (ll. 850–66)

FROM THE EXETER BOOK: *GUTHLAC B: THE DEATH OF ST. GUTHLAC OF CROWLAND*

This is one of two poems in the Exeter Book dealing with Guthlac, an Anglo-Saxon warrior of some prowess and renown who gave up his military career at age twenty-four to enter a monastery and eventually become a hermit in the fens of Crowland (d. Easter Wednesday, 714).[25] It is loosely based on the *Vita S. Guthlaci* (*Life of Saint Guthlac*), particularly chapter 50, by Felix, a writer otherwise unknown.[26] It recounts the final seven days of the saint's life and his interaction with his faithful, grieving follower (named Beccel in the Latin *Vita,* though never named in the Old English poem), who reluctantly watches the saint die. The poem begins with a disquisition on the origin of death in Adam and Eve's sin and of death's inevitability for everyone and every thing born into the world. But during its course, the poem makes clear that death is the pathway for Guthlac away from the hardship of this life into eternal bliss, not something that should be lamented. Before dying, Guthlac speaks compassionately with his companion, opens his mouth and exhales a honey-sweet breath that comforts his servant:

> At times he drew breath brave in strength; from his mouth came the sweetest of scents. As in the summer time blossoming plants in some places, flowing with honey, held fast by their roots, smell sweetly on the plains, so was the breath of the holy one drawn up all day long until evening. (ll. 1271–77)

Guthlac, who provides the perfect example of steadfast faith, becomes less the object of interest in this poem for the reader, however, than does his fallible servant, who serves as a painful reflection of our mutable selves. Like him, we frequently lack the spiritual steadfastness to willingly and happily let go of loved ones who must leave us at the end of life. The poem lacks its conclusion, and "a page or more may well have been lost from that poem, enough, for example, for a runic signature" from Cynewulf.[27]

FROM THE EXETER BOOK: *JULIANA: THE MARTYRDOM OF ST. JULIANA OF NICOMEDIA*

Like *The Fates of the Apostles,* and largely because of what some once considered its plain and uninteresting style, this poem about the early fourth-century St. Juliana of Nicomedia has been regarded as Cynewulf's first or his last work, the product of immaturity or of decline. It is, however, much more sophisticated and artful, especially in its use of direct discourse, than early critics gave it credit for, and as one of

two substantial poems by Cynewulf with a woman as pro-
tagonist, it commands our attention. That it may have been
written specifically to inspire a female religious audience in
the face of male hostility (perhaps the Danish invasions), as
many now assume, makes it an even more attractive object
of study.[28]

The poem is the earliest extant vernacular version of this
saint's life, and Cynewulf's source for it resembles a Latin
prose life in the *Acta Sanctorum* (*Acts of the Saints*) for Febru-
ary 16, although no precise source has been found.[29] The
young virgin, Juliana, is promised in marriage by her father,
Affricanus, to the pagan prefect Heliseus. She refuses the
bond unless Heliseus converts to Christianity; he refuses to
convert and imprisons her. She is tortured, tempted by a de-
mon, and finally beheaded. Cynewulf shifts the dynamics
found in his Latin source by making the saint and her oppo-
nents absolutely dichotomous. In the Latin, for example,
Heliseus says, "My Lady Juliana, give in to me and I will be-
lieve in your God," then hesitates because "if I do, the em-
peror will hear about it" and will relieve him of both his du-
ties and his head.[30] Cynewulf eliminates that scene and all
others that show evil or good equivocating. Yet he expands
direct discourse considerably in order to emphasize the
saint's attachment to the Logos, to Christ, and her separa-
tion from her ungodly persecutors.[31] Her lengthy confronta-
tion in the climax of the poem with the most wicked and
powerful of those persecutors, the demon, is almost entirely
verbal; after she grabs him (l. 288), she forces him to tell the
truth about all his evil deeds since the beginning of creation.
Cynewulf breaks up his signature into three groups (ᚳᚣᚾ
[CYN], ᛖᚹᚢ [EWU], ᛚᚠ [LF]), perhaps reflecting the anxi-

ety he must feel at the prospect of his own soul's eventual separation from the body that houses it.[32]

FROM THE VERCELLI BOOK: *FATES OF THE APOSTLES*

This catalog poem[33] lists the twelve apostles with succinct summaries about what they accomplished and how they died. Even though the Vercelli Book was first transcribed in 1834, scholars did not realize that *The Fates of the Apostles* was Cynewulf's until A. S. Napier published his edition of it, including the signature, in 1889.[34] Once it was attributed to Cynewulf, it attracted more attention than many critics thought it deserved; recent criticism has treated the poem more generously and has found literary merit in it.[35] Perhaps deriving from a martyrology or litany or passionary, but with no definite Latin source,[36] the poem—like *Juliana*—has been considered either Cynewulf's first or his last on the assumption that he was either just learning his craft or just losing it.[37] The arrangement of the letters in Cynewulf's name with the last letter appearing first is unique to this poem (ᚠ ᚱ ᚾ ᚱ ᚲ ᚪ ᛏ as *FWULCYN*), and Calder argues that "in breaking his name, [Cynewulf] begins the parting of soul from body."[38] The signature is thus tied to a central thematic concern.

FROM THE VERCELLI BOOK: *ELENE:*
THE FINDING OF THE TRUE CROSS

St. Helena (d. ca. 330) was the mother of Constantine the Great, the first Christian Roman emperor (d. 337), who brought tolerance for and imperial favor to Christianity. According to legend, Constantine defeated his enemy Maxentius in a battle at the Milvian Bridge by fighting under the sign of the cross; he had been instructed to do so in a dream, and the experience converted him to Christianity. He subsequently sent his mother on a mission to Jerusalem to find the True Cross, and that mission is the subject of Cynewulf's fine poetic rendition of a Latin source that closely resembles the *Acta Cyriaci* (*Acts of Cyriacus*) in the *Acta Sanctorum* for May 4.[39] Elene, portrayed as an Anglo-Saxon warrior queen in Cynewulf's poem, interrogates the Jews about where the cross is; their spokesperson, Judas, refuses to cooperate, and he is thrown into a pit for punishment, which quickly makes him relent. He converts to Christianity. One of his subsequent prayers produces a sign that indicates where the cross is, and another—after he becomes Cyriacus, the bishop of Jerusalem—brings a second sign about where the nails of the cross are. Once found, they are made into a bit for Constantine's horse. The poem's major themes have to do with revelation (of the cross, of the nails, and of Christian truths) and subsequent conversion (of Constantine, of Judas, of Cynewulf, and of the reader).[40] As in *Juliana,* Cynewulf expands direct discourse a great deal in the poem in order to promote his themes and emphasize the immutability of Elene's faith, rooted in the Logos, in the Word, in Christ.[41] As in *Juliana* and *Christ II* as well, Cynewulf reshapes his Mediterranean source and adds striking and memorable scenes to make the poem both decidedly Anglo-Saxon and clearly his. The opening, spirited battle scene (ll. 18–147), for example, is unlike any other passage in Cynewulf's work in its deployment of the lexis and imagery of Old English heroic poetry, right down to beasts of battle (the wolf and the eagle) waiting to feast on slain warriors. It is quickly followed (ll. 214–55) by a depiction of Elene as a heroic warlord-queen leading fierce fighters on a speedy sea journey reminiscent of Beowulf's to Denmark.[42] And the poem concludes (ll. 1276–1321) with an apocalyptic vision, in which God consigns all human beings into the embrace of the fire for the final conversion of repentant sinners into the eternally blessed and of cursed sinners and false tyrants into the eternally damned. One can easily see why many critics regard *Elene* as Cynewulf's best composition. But there is no reason to pick and choose: the five poems in this volume show that Cynewulf's poetry deserves our attention for its manifold aesthetic and intellectual virtues. It is inventive, its rhetoric is supple and compelling, it creates a sense of drama, and it achieves a fine balance, as Cædmon had before Cynewulf, between the Old English vernacular tradition and the Latin Christian message embodied in the verse. The poems render the message of the faith immediately accessible to fellow Anglo-Saxons as it engages their respect for the past and their need for an eternal, sanctified future.

I am indebted to a number of people and institutions for making this volume possible. John M. Hill originally invited me to produce a similar book for another series that subsequently ceased publication; Daniel Donoghue agreed to let me reshape that book to fit the requirements of the Dumbarton Oaks Medieval Library; and he, R. D. Fulk, and Elizabeth Tyler supplied excellent suggestions for improving the manuscript after I submitted it to the press. This is a much better book for the attention they paid to it. I am also grateful for two years of research leave, one at the Institute for Advanced Study, Princeton (2004–5), and the other at my home in Scottsdale, sponsored by the National Endowment for the Humanities (2006–7), during which time I was able to complete a great deal of work on this project while laboring on two others.

I dedicate this volume to my daughter, Francesca Erica Bjork, *min þæt swæse bearn.*

Notes

1 Bredehoft, *Authors,* 5–6, counts eight famous writers and about the same number of obscure ones.

2 George Hardin Brown, *A Companion to Bede* (Woodbridge, 2009), 15, 93.

3 *Complete Prose Works of John Milton,* vol. 1 (New Haven, 1953), 381.

4 He makes no comment at all on the runes at the ends of *Christ II* and *Juliana.* See S. A. J. Bradley, *N. S. F. Grundtvig's Transcriptions of the Exeter Book: An Analysis* (Copenhagen, 1998), 32, 40.

5 Calder, *Cynewulf,* 14, 18.

6 See Fulk, "Cynewulf," 10–15.

7 See Calder, *Cynewulf,* 15–18; Anderson, *Cynewulf,* 15.

8 Anderson, *Cynewulf,* 16.

9 Stodnick, "Cynewulf as Author."

10 See, for example, Donoghue, *Style,* 112–16, and Puskar, *"Hwa þas fitte fegde?"*

11 For a discussion of the use of runes by the Anglo-Saxons, see Page, *Introduction to Old English Runes.* He deals with Cynewulf's use of them on 191–97.

12 Frese, "Art of Cynewulf's Runic Signatures," 323.

13 Sisam, *Studies,* 23–26.

14 T. A. Shippey, *Old English Verse* (London, 1972), 156–58.

15 Donoghue, *Style,* 116; Bredehoft, *Authors,* 46.

16 Woolf, *Juliana,* 8.

17 See Niles, "Cynewulf's Initialisms," for a recent attempt to decipher the signature.

18 See Fulk, "Cynewulf," 15–16.

19 See ibid., 15.

20 See Sisam, *Studies,* 119–39 at 134; Roberts, *The Guthlac Poems,* 60–62; Fulk, "Cynewulf," 5; and Orchard, "Both Style and Substance," 272–73.

21 See Bjork, *Old English Verse Saints' Lives,* 90–109.

22 Chase, "God's Presence," 100.

23 Bent Noack, "Grundtvig and Anglo-Saxon Poetry," in *Heritage and Prophecy: Grundtvig and the English-Speaking World,* ed. A. M. Allchin, et al. (Aarhus, 1993), 40.

24 Calder, *Cynewulf,* p. 42; Allen and Calder, *Sources and Analogues,* 78–83.

25 On his reputation, see Colgrave, *Felix's Life of Saint Guthlac,* 3. On the relationship of Guthlac's day of death to major themes in the poem, see Lucas, "Easter, the Death of Guthlac."

26 See Colgrave, *Felix's Life of Saint Guthlac* for an edition of the Latin life. For the use Cynewulf made of this source, see Roberts, *The Guthlac Poems,* 36; Allen and Calder, *Sources and Analogues,* 109–12.

27 Krapp and Dobbie, *The Exeter Book,* xxxii. See also Roberts, *The Guthlac Poems,* 47–48, and Muir, *The Exeter Anthology,* vol. 1, 12.

28 See, e.g., Horner, *Discourse of Enclosure,* 104–7. For a review of some of the evidence for female literacy in Anglo-Saxon England, see Brown, "Female Book-Ownership."

29 Allen and Calder, *Sources and Analogues,* 122–32.

30 Ibid., 124.

31 See Bjork, *Old English Verse Saints' Lives,* 45–61.

32 Calder, *Cynewulf,* 103.

33 See Howe, *Old English Catalogue Poems.*

34 "Collation der altengl. Gedichte im Vercellibuch." Haupt's *Zeitschrift für deutsches Altertum* 33 (1889): 66–73.

35 For older views, see Calder, *Cynewulf,* 29. For the more recent reassessment, see, for example, Boren, "Form and Meaning"; Hieatt, "Imagery, Structure, and Meaning"; Cross, "Cynewulf's Traditions"; and Rice, "Penitential Motif."

36 See McCulloh, "Did Cynewulf Use a Martyrology?," 81–83.

37 First: Woolf, *Juliana,* 7; last: Schaar, *Critical Studies,* 261.

38 Calder, *Cynewulf,* 38.

39 Allen and Calder, *Sources and Analogues,* 59–69.

40 See especially Campbell, "Cynewulf's Multiple Revelations."

41 See Bjork, *Old English Verse Saints' Lives,* 62–89.

42 For a recent and balanced discussion of the question of Elene's female agency in this poem, see Klein, *Ruling Women,* 53–85.

CHRIST II

The Ascension

440 Nu ðu geornlice   gæst-gerynum,
mon se mæra,   mod-cræfte sec
þurh sefan snyttro,   þæt þu soð wite
hu þæt geeode,   þa se ælmihtiga
acenned wearð   þurh clænne had,
445 siþþan he Marian,   mægða weolman,
mærre meowlan,   mund-heals geceas,
þæt þær in hwitum   hræglum gewerede
englas ne oðeowdun,   þa se æþeling cwom,
beorn in Betlem.   Bodan wæron gearwe
450 þa þurh hleoþor-cwide   hyrdum cyðdon,
sægdon soðne gefean,   þætte Sunu wære
in middan-geard   meotudes acenned,
in Betleme.   Hwæþre in bocum ne cwið
þæt hy in hwitum   þær hræglum oðywden
455 in þa æþelan tid,   swa hie eft dydon
ða se brega mæra   to Bethania,
þeoden þrymfæst,   his þegna gedryht
gelaðade, leof weorud.   Hy þæs lareowes
on þam wil-dæge   word ne gehyrwdon,
460 hyra sinc-giefan.   Sona wæron gearwe,
hæleð mid Hlaford,   to þære halgan byrg,
þær him tacna fela   tires brytta
onwrah, wuldres helm,   word-gerynum,
ærþon up stige   an-cenned Sunu,

Now, excellent man, in spiritual mysteries   440
earnestly seek with strength of mind,
through wisdom of heart, so that you may
know the truth about why it was
when the almighty was born in purity,
when he chose protection within Mary,   445
the selected maiden, the famous virgin,
that angels did not appear there clad
in white garments when the prince, the man,
came to Bethlehem. Ready were the messengers
who through speech to the shepherds   450
announced, proclaimed the true
joy, that the Son of the creator was born in
middle-earth in Bethlehem. However, in books it
does not say that they appeared in white
garments at that noble hour as they later did   455
when the famous ruler, the glorious prince,
summoned his band of servants, the dear
troop, to Bethany. They did not despise
the words of the teacher, of their treasure giver,
on that day of joy. They, the warriors with the Lord,   460
were ready at once to go to the holy city,
where the dispenser of fame, the protector of glory,
revealed to them many signs, deep sayings,
before he, the only-begotten Son, the child

465 efen-ece bearn,   agnum Fæder,
þæs ymb feowertig   þe he of foldan ær
from deaðe aras,   dagena rimes.
Hæfde þa gefylled,   swa ær biforan sungon,
witgena word   geond woruld innan
470 þurh his þrowinga.   Þegnas heredon,
lufedun leofwendum   lifes agend,
Fæder frum-sceafta.   He him fægre þæs,
leofum gesiþum,   lean æfter geaf,
ond þæt word acwæð   waldend engla,
475 gefysed, Frea mihtig,   to Fæder rice:
"Gefeoð ge on ferððe.   Næfre ic from hweorfe,
ac ic lufan symle   læste wið eowic,
ond eow meaht giefe   ond mid wunige,
awo to ealdre,   þæt eow æfre ne bið
480 þurh gife mine   godes onsien.
Farað nu geond ealne   yrmenne grund,
geond wid-wegas,   weoredum cyðað,
bodiað ond bremað   beorhtne geleafan,
ond fulwiað   folc under roderum,
485 hweorfað to heofonum.   Hergas breotaþ,
fyllað ond feogað,   feondscype dwæscað,
sibbe sawað   on sefan manna
þurh meahta sped.   Ic eow mid wunige
forð on frofre   ond eow friðe healde
490 strengðu staþolfæstre   on stowa gehware."
Ða wearð semninga   sweg on lyfte
hlud gehyred.   Heofon-engla þreat,
weorud wlite-scyne,   wuldres aras,

eternal equally with his own Father, ascended   465
after forty of the count of days from his death
that he had risen from the earth.
He had fulfilled, as they had sung before,
the words of the prophets within the world
through his sufferings. The servants praised,   470
pleasantly honored the master of life,
the Father of first creation. He gave them,
the beloved companions, a fair reward afterward for that
and spoke these words, the ruler of angels,
the mighty Lord, ready to travel to his Father's kingdom: 475
"Be glad in heart. I will never turn away
but will always keep loving you
and give you power and dwell with you,
always and forever, so that through my grace
you will never be lacking in good.   480
Go now throughout all the whole earth,
through the distant regions, make known to the
multitudes, preach and proclaim the bright faith,
and baptize people under the firmament,
turn them to the heavens. Smash their idols,   485
lay them low and hate them, extinguish deviltry,
sow peace in the people's hearts
through the abundance of your powers. I will dwell with
you as a comfort from now on and hold you in peace
with a steadfast strength everywhere."   490
Then suddenly a loud noise was heard
in the sky. A throng of heavenly angels,
a beautiful host, arose from glory,

cwomun on corðre.   Cyning ure gewat
495 þurh þæs temples hrof   þær hy to segun,
þa þe leofes þa gen   last weardedun
on þam þing-stede,   þegnas gecorene.
Gesegon hi on heahþu   Hlaford stigan,
God-Bearn of grundum.   Him wæs geomor sefa
500 hat æt heortan,   hyge murnende,
þæs þe hi swa leofne   leng ne mostun
geseon under swegle.   Song ahofun
aras ufancunde,   æþeling heredun,
lofedun lif-fruman,   leohte gefegun
505 þe of þæs hælendes   heafelan lixte.
Gesegon hy ælbeorhte   englas twegen
fægre ymb þæt frum-bearn   frætwum blican,
cyninga wuldor.   Cleopedon of heahþu
wordum wrætlicum   ofer wera mengu
510 beorhtan reorde: "Hwæt bidað ge,
Galilesce   guman on hwearfte?
Nu ge sweotule geseoð   soðne Dryhten
on swegl faran;   sigores agend
wile up heonan   eard gestigan,
515 æþelinga ord,   mid þas engla gedryht,
ealra folca fruma,   Fæder eþel-stoll.
We mid þyslice   þreate willað
ofer heofona gehlidu   Hlaford fergan
to þære beorhtan byrg   mid þas bliðan gedryht,
520 ealra sige-bearna   þæt seleste
ond æþeleste,   þe ge her on stariað
ond in frofre geseoð   frætwum blican.
Wile eft swa þeah   eorðan mægðe

came in a company. Our king departed
through the roof of the temple where they looked on,   495
those who still kept track of the beloved one
in that meeting place, the chosen attendants.
They saw the Lord ascend into the heights,
the divine Son from the ground. Their spirit was sad,
hot around the heart, their mind mourning,   500
because they no longer could see under heaven
the one so dear. The celestial messengers
raised up a song, praised the prince,
glorified the author of life, rejoiced in the light
that shone from the savior's head.   505
They saw two radiant angels
fair by that firstborn son, the glory of kings,
glowing in their array. They called from the heights
in wondrous words over the crowd of men
in a clear voice: "What are you waiting for,   510
men of Galilee, in a circle?
Now you clearly see the true Lord
go into heaven; the owner of victory, the chief
of princes, the creator of all peoples wants to ascend
with his band of angels from here to his home,   515
to the native seat of his Father.
With such a troop, with this happy host,
we will lead the Lord over the vault of the heavens
to that bright city, will lead
the best and noblest of all victory children   520
whom you look on here
and to your consolation see glowing in his array.
He himself nevertheless will seek again

sylfa gesecan   side herge,
525 ond þonne gedeman   dæda gehwylce
þara ðe gefremedon   folc under roderum."
Ða wæs wuldres weard   wolcnum bifongen,
heah-engla cyning,   ofer hrofas upp,
haligra helm.   Hyht wæs geniwad,
530 blis in burgum,   þurh þæs beornes cyme.
Gesæt sige-hremig   on þa swiþran hand
ece ead-fruma   agnum Fæder.
Gewitan him þa gongan   to Hierusalem
hæleð hyge-rofe,   in þa halgan burg,
535 geomor-mode,   þonan hy God nyhst
up stigende   eagum segun,
hyra wil-gifan.   Þær wæs wopes hring;
torne bitolden   wæs seo treow-lufu
hat æt heortan,   hreðer innan weoll,
540 beorn breost-sefa.   Bidon ealle þær
þegnas þrymfulle   þeodnes gehata
in þære torhtan   byrig tyn niht þa gen,
swa him sylf bibead   swegles Agend,
ærþon up stige   ealles waldend
545 on heofona gehyld.   Hwite cwoman
eorla ead-giefan   englas togeanes.
Ðæt is wel cweden,   swa gewritu secgað,
þæt him al-beorhte   englas togeanes
in þa halgan tid   heapum cwoman,
550 sigan on swegle.   Þa wæs symbla mæst
geworden in wuldre.   Wel þæt gedafenað
þæt to þære blisse,   beorhte gewerede,
in þæs þeodnes burg   þegnas cwoman,
weorud wlite-scyne.   Gesegon wil-cuman

the nations of earth with a great army,
and then judge each deed   525
that people have done under the firmament."
Then the guardian of glory, the king of the archangels,
the protector of the saints, was enveloped in clouds
above the roofs. Hope was renewed,
bliss in the cities through the coming of the man.   530
Triumphant, the eternal source of joy sat
at the right hand of his own Father.
Then the stouthearted warriors, sad at heart, set out
from where with their own eyes they had just seen God,
their gracious giver, ascending   535
to walk to Jerusalem, into
the holy city. There was the sound of lamentation;
overwhelmed with grief, constant love was
hot around the heart, the breast raged within,
the soul burned. There all the glorious attendants   540
waited the prince's promise
for ten more nights in that bright city,
as he himself, the Lord of heaven, commanded,
before the ruler of all ascended
into the keeping of the heavens. Shining angels   545
came toward men's giver of happiness.
That is well declared, as the scriptures say,
that radiant angels in throngs descending
from the sky came toward him
in that holy hour. Then was the greatest of feasts   550
made in glory. It is well fitting
that into that bliss, brightly arrayed,
into the city of the prince his attendants came,
the beautiful host. The welcome ones saw

9

555 on heah-setle   heofones waldend,
folca feorh-giefan,   frætwum . . .

. . . ealles waldend
middan-geardes   ond mægen-þrymmes.
"Hafað nu se halga   helle bireafod
ealles þæs gafoles   þe hi gear-dagum
560 in þæt orlege   unryhte swealg.
Nu sind forcumene   ond in cwic-susle
gehynde ond gehæfte,   in helle grund
duguþum bidæled,   deofla cempan.
Ne meahtan wiþerbrogan   wige spowan,
565 wæpna wyrpum,   siþþan wuldres cyning,
heofon-rices helm,   hilde gefremede
wiþ his eald-feondum   anes meahtum;
þær he of hæfte ahlod   huþa mæste
of feonda byrig,   folces unrim,
570 þisne ilcan þreat   þe ge her on stariað.
Wile nu gesecan   sawla nergend
gæsta gief-stol,   Godes agen bearn,
æfter guð-plegan.   Nu ge geare cunnon
hwæt se Hlaford is   se þisne here lædeð,
575 nu ge fromlice   freondum togeanes
gongað glæd-mode.   Geatu ontynað!
Wile in to eow   ealles waldend,
cyning on ceastre,   corðre ne lytle,
fyrn-weorca fruma,   folc gelædan
580 in dreama dream,   ðe he on deoflum genom
þurh his sylfes sygor.   Sib sceal gemæne
englum ond ældum   a forð heonan
wesan wide-ferh.   Wær is ætsomne

on his high seat the ruler of heaven,   555
life-giver of the people, in array . . .

                                        . . . the ruler of all
middle-earth and of the heavenly host.
"Now the holy one has deprived hell
of all the tribute that it in days of old
unjustly swallowed in that battle.   560
Now vanquished and in living torment,
scorned and confined, bereft of honors,
the devil-warriors are in the pit of hell.
His adversaries could not succeed in war,
in the hurling of weapons, after the king of glory,   565
the protector of the heavenly kingdom, engaged in battle
against his old foes through the power of one;
there from captivity he delivered the greatest of spoils
from the city of enemies, countless people,
this same troop that you look upon here.   570
The savior of souls, God's own child,
wants now to seek the gift-throne of spirits,
after the battle-play. Now that you clearly know
who the Lord is who leads this army,
go boldly, glad in heart,   575
toward the enemies. Open the gates!
The ruler of all wants to come in to you,
the king into the city with not a little troop,
the creator of ancient works, to lead the people
into the joy of joys, those whom he from the devils seized   580
through his own victories. There shall be
a common peace forever and ever hence forward
among angels and people. There is a united covenant

Godes ond monna, gæst-halig treow,
585 lufu, lifes hyht, ond ealles leohtes gefea."
Hwæt, we nu gehyrdan hu þæt hælu-bearn
þurh his hyder-cyme hals eft forgeaf,
gefreode ond gefreoþade folc under wolcnum,
mære meotudes Sunu, þæt nu monna gehwylc
590 cwic þendan her wunað, geceosan mot
swa helle hienþu swa heofones mærþu,
swa þæt leohte leoht swa ða laþan niht,
swa þrymmes þræce swa þystra wræce,
swa mid Dryhten dream swa mid deoflum hream,
595 swa wite mid wraþum swa wuldor mid arum,
swa lif swa deað, swa him leofre bið
to gefremmanne, þenden flæsc ond gæst
wuniað in worulde. Wuldor þæs age
þrynysse Þrym, þonc butan ende.
600 Ðæt is þæs wyrðe þætte wer-þeode
secgen Dryhtne þonc duguða gehwylcre
þe us sið ond ær simle gefremede
þurh monigfealdra mægna geryno.
He us æt giefeð ond æhta sped,
605 welan ofer wid-lond, ond weder liþe
under swegles hleo. Sunne ond mona,
æþelast tungla eallum scinað,
heofon-condelle, hæleþum on eorðan.
Dreoseð deaw ond ren, duguðe weccaþ
610 to feorhnere fira cynne,
iecað eorð-welan. Þæs we ealles sculon
secgan þonc ond lof þeodne ussum
ond huru þære hælo þe he us to hyhte forgeaf,

of God and human beings, a pledge holy in spirit,
love, hope of life, and joy of all light."   585
Listen, now we have heard how the salvation-child
through his incarnation gave redemption again,
freed and defended people below the clouds,
the illustrious Son of the measurer, so that each person
while dwelling here alive might choose   590
the ignominies of hell or the glories of heaven,
the beloved light or the hateful night,
the rush of the host or the punishment of the darknesses,
joy with the Lord or lamentation with devils,
torment with enemies or glory with angels,   595
life or death, whichever will be pleasing to him
to perform while flesh and spirit
dwell in the world. For that may the majesty of the Trinity
have glory, thanks without end.
It is fitting that the nations   600
should say thanks to the Lord for each of honors
that for us, early and late, he has always made
through the mystery of his manifold powers.
He gives us food and an abundance of possessions,
wealth across the wide land and pleasant weather   605
under the shelter of the sky. The sun and moon,
the noblest of stars, heaven's candles,
shine on all people on earth.
Dew and rain fall, summon benefits
for the sustenance of human kind,   610
increase the riches of the earth. For all of this, we must
give thanks and praise to our prince and especially
for that salvation that he gave to us as a hope,

ða he þa yrmpðu   eft oncyrde
615   æt his up-stige   þe we ær drugon,
ond geþingade   þeod-buendum
wið Fæder swæsne   fæhþa mæste,
cyning anboren.   Cwide eft onhwearf
saulum to sibbe,   se þe ær sungen wæs
620   þurh yrne hyge   ældum to sorge:
"Ic þec of eorðan geworhte,   on þære þu scealt yrmþum
                                            lifgan,

wunian in gewinne   ond wræce dreogan,
feondum to hroþor   fus-leoð galan,
ond to þære ilcan scealt   eft geweorþan,
625   wyrmum aweallen;   þonan wites fyr
of þære eorðan scealt   eft gesecan."
Hwæt, us þis se æþeling   yðre gefremede
þa he leomum onfeng   ond lic-homan,
monnes magu-tudre.   Siþþan meotodes Sunu
630   engla eþel   up gestigan
wolde, weoroda God,   us se willa bicwom
heanum to helpe   on þa halgan tid.
Bi þon giedd awræc   Iob, swa he cuðe,
herede helm wera,   hælend lofede,
635   ond mid sib-lufan   sunu waldendes
freo-noman cende,   ond hine fugel nemde,
þone Iudeas   ongietan ne meahtan
in ðære godcundan   gæstes strengðu.
Wæs þæs fugles flyht   feondum on eorþan
640   dyrne ond degol,   þam þe deorc gewit
hæfdon on hreþre,   heortan stænne.
Noldan hi þa torhtan   tacen oncnawan

when he, the only begotten king, ended the misery
at his ascension that we earlier suffered   615
and interceded for humankind
with the beloved Father in the
greatest of feuds. He reversed the decree
for the peace of souls that earlier was sung
through wrathful mind as a sorrow to human beings: 620
"I made you from earth, where you must live in misery,
dwell in strife and endure pain,
sing a death song as a pleasure to enemies,
and to the same you must return again,
swarming with worms; from there, from the earth,   625
you must then seek the fire of punishment."
Listen, the prince made this easier for us,
the human race, when he took on
limbs and body. Once the Son of the creator,
the God of hosts, wanted to ascend to the   630
homeland of angels, the desire came at the holy time
to help us wretched ones.
About that, Job, as he well could, recited a lay,
praised the protector of men, exalted the savior,
and with love assigned a surname to the son   635
of the ruler and called him a bird,
the one the Jews could not understand
in the strength of his divine spirit.
The flight of that bird was hidden and secret
from enemies on earth, from those who had dark   640
perception in their bosom, a stony heart.
They did not want to acknowledge the bright signs

þe him beforan fremede   Freo-Bearn Godes,
monig mislicu,   geond middan-geard.
645   Swa se fæla fugel   flyges cunnode;
hwilum engla eard   up gesohte,
modig meahtum strang,   þone maran ham,
hwilum he to eorþan   eft gestylde,
þurh gæstes giefe   grund-sceat sohte,
650   wende to worulde.   Bi þon se witga song:
"He wæs upp hafen   engla fæðmum
in his þa miclan   meahta spede,
heah ond halig,   ofer heofona þrym."
Ne meahtan þa þæs fugles   flyht gecnawan
655   þe þæs up-stiges   ondsæc fremedon,
ond þæt ne gelyfdon,   þætte lif-fruma
in monnes hiw   ofer mægna þrym,
halig from hrusan,   ahafen wurde.
Ða us geweorðade   se þas world gescop,
660   Godes gæst-sunu,   ond us giefe sealde,
uppe mid englum   ece staþelas,
ond eac monigfealde   modes snyttru
seow ond sette   geond sefan monna.
Sumum word-laþe   wise sendeð
665   on his modes gemynd   þurh his muþes gæst,
æðele ondgiet.   Se mæg eal fela
singan ond secgan   þam bið snyttru cræft
bifolen on ferðe.   Sum mæg fingrum wel
hlude fore hæleþum   hearpan stirgan,
670   gleo-beam gretan.   Sum mæg godcunde
reccan ryhte æ.   Sum mæg ryne tungla
secgan, side gesceaft.   Sum mæg searolice

that the noble Son of God made before them,
many and varied, throughout the earth.
So the faithful bird took flight;   645
sometimes upward he sought the abode of angels,
that famous home, courageous and strong in his
powers; sometimes he again rushed to earth, through
the gift of the spirit sought the region of the ground,
returned to the world. About that the prophet sang: 650
"He was raised up in the embrace of angels
in the great wealth of his powers,
lofty and holy, over the glory of the heavens."
They could not know the flight of the bird,
those who denied the ascension   655
and did not believe that the creator of life
was raised up in the shape of a man above the glory
of the hosts, holy from the earth.
Then he honored us, he who created this world,
the spiritual son of God, and gave us gifts,   660
eternal foundations up among the angels
and also sowed and established manifold
wisdom of mind throughout people's hearts.
To one he sends wise eloquence,
noble understanding, into his mind's memory through 665
the spirit of his mouth. The one in whom the craft of
wisdom is entrusted in the heart can sing and tell
very many things. One with fingers
can touch the harp well and loudly before the warriors,
play the joyous wood. One can rightly expound   670
the divine law. One can determine the course of the stars,
the broad creation. One can skillfully

word-cwide writan.   Sumum wiges sped
giefeð æt guþe,   þonne gar-getrum
675   ofer scild-hreadan   sceotend sendað,
flacor flan-geweorc.   Sum mæg fromlice
ofer sealtne sæ   sund-wudu drifan,
hreran holm-þræce.   Sum mæg heanne beam
stælgne gestigan.   Sum mæg styled sweord,
680   wæpen gewyrcan.   Sum con wonga bigong,
wegas wid-gielle.   Swa se waldend us,
God-Bearn on grundum,   his giefe bryttað.
Nyle he ængum anum   ealle gesyllan
gæstes snyttru,   þy læs him gielp sceþþe
685   þurh his anes cræft   ofer oþre forð.
Ðus God meahtig   geofum unhneawum,
cyning al-wihta,   cræftum weorðaþ
eorþan tuddor;   swylce eadgum blæd
seleð on swegle,   sibbe ræreþ
690   ece to ealdre   engla ond monna;
swa he his weorc weorþað.   Bi þon se witga cwæð
þæt ahæfen wæren   halge gimmas,
hædre heofon-tungol,   healice upp,
sunne ond mona.   Hwæt sindan þa
695   gimmas swa scyne   buton God sylfa?
He is se soðfæsta   sunnan leoma,
englum ond eorð-warum   æþele scima.
Ofer middan-geard   mona lixeð,
gæstlic tungol,   swa seo Godes circe
700   þurh gesomninga   soðes ond ryhtes
beorhte bliceð.   Swa hit on bocum cwiþ,
siþþan of grundum   God-Bearn astag,
cyning clænra gehwæs,   þa seo circe her

write discourse. To one he gives success
in battle when archers send
a shower of darts over the shields,   675
flights of arrows. One can confidently
drive the ship over the salt sea,
stir the raging billow. One can ascend
the tall, steep tree. One can make a hardened
sword, a weapon. One knows the course of the plains,   680
the far-reaching paths. Thus to us the ruler,
the Son of God on earth, dispenses gifts.
He does not want to give to anyone
complete wisdom of spirit lest pride should harm him
because of his singular skill above others.   685
Thus mighty God through bounteous gifts,
the king of all creatures, makes worthy with skills
the offspring of the earth; he also gives glory
to the blessed in the sky, ordains peace
for ever and ever for angels and humans;   690
thus he honors his work. About that the prophet said
that the holy gems were raised up on high,
the brilliant heavenly stars,
the sun and the moon. Why are those
gems so bright unless they are God himself?   695
He is the true light of the sun,
for angels and earth-dwellers, a noble radiance.
Over middle-earth the moon shines,
the spiritual star, as the church of God
brightly beams through the joining of   700
truth and right. Thus it says in books,
after the Son of God, the king of every pure thing,
ascended from the earth, the church

æ-fyllendra   eahtnysse bad
705   under hæþenra   hyrda gewealdum.
Þær ða syn-sceaðan   soþes ne giemdon,
gæstes þearfe,   ac hi Godes tempel
bræcan ond bærndon,   blod-gyte worhtan,
feodan ond fyldon.   Hwæþre forð bicwom
710   þurh Gæstes giefe   Godes þegna blæd
æfter up-stige   ecan Dryhtnes.
Bi þon Salomon song,   sunu Dauiþes,
giedda gearo-snottor   gæst-gerynum,
waldend wer-þeoda,   ond þæt word acwæð:
715   "Cuð þæt geweorðeð,   þætte cyning engla,
meotud meahtum swið,   munt gestylleð,
gehleapeð hea dune,   hyllas ond cnollas
bewrið mid his wuldre,   woruld alyseð,
ealle eorð-buend,   þurh þone æþelan styll."
720   Wæs se forma hlyp   þa he on fæmnan astag,
mæged unmæle,   ond þær mennisc hiw
onfeng butan firenum   þæt to frofre gewearð
eallum eorð-warum.   Wæs se oþer stiell
bearnes gebyrda,   þa he in binne wæs
725   in cildes hiw   claþum bewunden,
ealra þrymma þrym.   Wæs se þridda hlyp,
rodor-cyninges ræs,   þa he on rode astag,
Fæder, frofre Gæst.   Wæs se feorða stiell
in byrgenne,   þa he þone beam ofgeaf,
730   fold-ærne fæst.   Wæs se fifta hlyp
þa he hell-warena   heap forbygde

here suffered the persecution of the law destroyers
under the power of heathen rulers.   705
The evildoers there were not mindful of the truth,
the need of the Spirit, but they shattered and burned
the temples of God, shed blood,
hated and destroyed. However, through the gift
of the spirit, the glory of God's attendants came forth   710
after the ascension of the eternal Lord.
About that Solomon, the son of David,
very wise in poems, ruler of nations,
sang through meditations and said these words:
"It will become known that the king of angels,   715
the creator strong in his powers, will jump upon the
mountain, leap upon the high downs, envelop hills
and knolls with his glory, redeem the world,
all earth-dwellers, through that noble jump."
The first leap was when he descended into a woman,   720
an unblemished maiden, and there took on
human form without sin; that became a comfort
for all earth's inhabitants. The second jump was
the birth of the son when he in the manger
in the form of a child was wrapped in clothes,   725
the glory of all glories. The third leap, the bounding
of the heavenly king, was when he, the Father,
the comforting Spirit, ascended the cross. The fourth
jump was into the tomb, when he gave up the tree,
fast in the grave. The fifth leap was   730
when he brought low the troop of hell dwellers

in cwic-susle,   cyning inne gebond,
feonda fore-sprecan,   fyrnum teagum,
grom-hydigne,   þær he gen ligeð
735   in carcerne   clommum gefæstnad,
synnum gesæled.   Wæs se siexta hlyp,
haliges hyht-plega,   þa he to heofonum astag
on his eald-cyððe.   Þa wæs engla þreat
on þa halgan tid   hleahtre bliþe
740   wynnum geworden.   Gesawan wuldres þrym,
æþelinga ord,   eðles neosan,
beorhtra bolda.   Þa wearð burg-warum
eadgum ece gefea   æþelinges plega.
Þus her on grundum   Godes ece Bearn
745   ofer heah-hleoþu   hlypum stylde,
modig æfter muntum.   Swa we men sculon
heortan gehygdum   hlypum styllan
of mægne in mægen,   mærþum tilgan
þæt we to þam hyhstan   hrofe gestigan
750   halgum weorcum,   þær is hyht ond blis,
geþungen þegn-weorud.   Is us þearf micel
þæt we mid heortan   hælo secen,
þær we mid gæste   georne gelyfað
þæt þæt hælo-bearn   heonan up stige
755   mid usse lic-homan,   lifgende God.
Forþon we a sculon   idle lustas,
syn-wunde forseon,   ond þæs sellran gefeon.
Habbað we us to frofre   Fæder on roderum
ælmeahtigne.   He his aras þonan,
760   halig of heahðu,   hider onsendeð,
þa us gescildaþ   wið sceþþendra

in living torment, bound the king within,
the spokesman of the enemies, with fiery fetters,
the fierce one, where he still lies
in prison fastened with chains,   735
shackled with sins. The sixth leap,
the joyous play of the holy one, was when he ascended to
heaven to his old home. Then the host of angels
in that holy hour was made happy with rapture,
with joy. They saw glory's majesty,   740
the chief of princes, seek his homeland,
the bright dwellings. Then for the blessed city dwellers
the play of the prince became an eternal delight.
Thus here on earth God's eternal Son
sprang in leaps over the lofty hills,   745
courageous over the mountains. So must we humans
in the thoughts of our hearts spring in leaps
from strength to strength, strive for glorious deeds
so that we may ascend to the highest summit
through holy works where there is hope and bliss,   750
a perfect host of attendants. The need is great for us
that we should seek salvation with our heart,
where we with our spirit readily believe
that that child bringing salvation, the living God,
will ascend from here with our body.   755
Therefore we must always despise idle desires,
the wounds of sin, and rejoice in the better part.
As a comfort for us, we have the almighty Father
in the firmament. He sends his messengers,
holy from the heights, from there to here,   760
who shield us against the deadly arrow attacks

eglum earh-farum,   þi læs unholdan
wunde gewyrcen,   þonne wroht-bora
in folc Godes   forð onsendeð
765 of his brægd-bogan   biterne stræl.
Forþon we fæste sculon   wið þam fær-scyte
symle wærlice   wearde healdan,
þy læs se attres ord   in gebuge,
biter bord-gelac,   under ban-locan,
770 feonda fær-searo.   Þæt bið frecne wund,
blatast benna.   Utan us beorgan þa,
þenden we on eorðan   eard weardien;
utan us to Fæder   freoþa wilnian,
biddan Bearn Godes   ond þone bliðan Gæst
775 þæt he us gescilde   wið sceaþan wæpnum,
laþra lyge-searwum,   se us lif forgeaf,
leomu, lic ond gæst.   Si him lof symle
þurh woruld worulda,   wuldor on heofnum.
Ne þearf him ondrædan   deofla strælas
780 ænig on eorðan   ælda cynnes,
gromra garfare,   gif hine God scildeþ,
duguða Dryhten.   Is þam dome neah
þæt we gelice sceolon   leanum hleotan,
swa we wide-feorh   weorcum hlodun
785 geond sidne grund.   Us secgað bec
hu æt ærestan   ead-mod astag
in middan-geard   mægna gold-hord,
in fæmnan fæðm   freo-bearn Godes,

of the evildoers, lest the fiends
should inflict wounds when the author of evil
sends forth among the people of God
from his deceitful bow a biting shaft.   765
Therefore we must always firmly and cautiously
hold guard against the sudden shot
lest the poisoned point should penetrate, the biting
missile that flies against the shield, into the body,
the sudden device of enemies. That is a dangerous   770
wound, the most livid of lesions. Let us then defend
ourselves, while we inhabit a dwelling on earth;
let us entreat the Father for refuge,
implore the Son of God and the merciful Spirit
that he should shield us from the weapons of foes,   775
the wiles of enemies, he who gave us life,
limbs, body, and spirit. Praise be to him always
and forever, glory in the heavens.
There is no need for anyone in the human race
on earth to dread the devil's darts,   780
the spear flights of the fierce ones, if God, the Lord of
hosts, shields him or her. That judgment is near
when we have to receive rewards equal to what
we earned during life through works
throughout the wide ground. Books tell us   785
how at first the gold-hoard of strengths descended
humble into middle-earth, the noble child of God,
holy from the heights, into the womb

halig of heahþu.   Huru ic wene me
790   ond eac ondræde   dom ðy reþran,
ðonne eft cymeð   engla þeoden,
þe ic ne heold teala   þæt me hælend min
on bocum bibead.   Ic þæs brogan sceal
geseon syn-wræce,   þæs þe ic soð talge,
795   þær monig beoð   on gemot læded
fore onsyne   eces deman.
Þonne ᚳ cwacað,   gehyreð cyning mæðlan,
rodera ryhtend,   sprecan reþe word
þam þe him ær in worulde   wace hyrdon,
800   þendan ᛁ ond ᚠ   yþast meahtan
frofre findan.   Þær sceal forht monig
on þam wong-stede   werig bidan
hwæt him æfter dædum   deman wille
wraþra wita.   Biþ se ᛚ scæcen
805   eorþan frætwa.   ᚢ wæs longe
ᛚ-flodum bilocen,   lif-wynna dæl,
ᚹ on foldan.   Þonne frætwe sculon
byrnan on bæle;   blac rasetteð
recen reada leg,   reþe scriþeð
810   geond woruld wide.   Wongas hreosað,
burg-stede berstað.   Brond bið on tyhte,
æleð eald-gestreon   unmurnlice,
gæsta gifrast,   þæt geo guman heoldan,
þenden him on eorþan   onmedla wæs.
815   Forþon ic leofra gehwone   læran wille
þæt he ne agæle   gæstes þearfe,
ne on gylp geote,   þenden God wille

26

of the virgin. Indeed, I expect and also dread
for myself a sterner judgment,   790
when the prince of angels comes again,
because I did not hold well what my savior
commanded me in books. For that, I have to see terror,
punishment, as I truly believe,
where many will be led into assembly   795
before the visage of the eternal judge.
Then ᚲ will quake, will hear the king speak,
the ruler of the heavens utter stern words
to those who feebly obeyed him in the world,
while ᚼ and ᛏ could most easily   800
find comfort. Many, afraid and accursed,
must wait there in that place to hear what horrible
punishments he will assign them according to their deeds.
The ᚠ of the treasures of earth
will have fled. ᚾ share of life-joys was long   805
shut in by the ᛁ-streams,
our ᚹ on earth. Then the treasures must
burn on the pyre; bright will rage
the swift red flame, will quickly glide
throughout the wide world. The plains will fall,   810
the city-places burst asunder. The conflagration, the
greediest of spirits, will be in motion, will relentlessly
consume the ancient treasures that men once held
while pride was theirs on earth.
Therefore I want to teach each of loved ones   815
not to neglect the need of the spirit,
nor dissipate it in boasting, while God wills

27

þæt he her in worulde   wunian mote,
somed siþian   sawel in lice,
820 in þam gæst-hofe.   Scyle gumena gehwylc
on his gear-dagum   georne biþencan
þæt us milde bicwom   meahta waldend
æt ærestan   þurh þæs engles word.
Bið nu eorneste   þonne eft cymeð,
825 reðe ond ryht-wis.   Rodor bið onhrered,
ond þas miclan gemetu   middan-geardes
beofiað þonne.   Beorht cyning leanað
þæs þe hy on eorþan   eargum dædum
lifdon leahtrum fa.   Þæs hi longe sculon
830 ferð-werige onfon   in fyr-baðe,
wælmum biwrecene,   wraþlic ondlean,
þonne mægna cyning   on gemot cymeð,
þrymma mæste.   Þeod-egsa bið
hlud gehyred   bi heofon-woman,
835 cwaniendra cirm,   cerge reotað
fore onsyne   eces deman,
þa þe hyra weorcum   wace truwiað.
Ðær biþ oðywed   egsa mara
þonne from frum-gesceape   gefrægen wurde
840 æfre on eorðan.   Þær bið æghwylcum
syn-wyrcendra   on þa snudan tid
leofra micle   þonne eall þeos læne gesceaft,
þær he hine sylfne   on þam sige-þreate
behydan mæge,   þonne herga Fruma,
845 æþelinga ord,   eallum demeð,
leofum ge laðum,   lean æfter ryhte,
þeoda gehwylcre.   Is us þearf micel

that he or she dwell here in the world,
journey with the soul together in the body,
in that guesthouse. All in our   820
lifetime must earnestly keep in mind
that the ruler of powers came graciously to us
at first through the word of an angel.
He will be stern when he comes again,
fierce and righteous. The firmament will be shaken,   825
and the great boundaries of middle-earth
will tremble. The bright king will reward
them because they lived on earth through wicked deeds,
stained with vices. For a long time for that,
soul-weary they have to suffer in a bath of fire,   830
surrounded by its surgings, dire retribution,
when the king of powers comes to the assembly,
the greatest of glories. The terror of the people will be
heard loud along with the sound from the heavens,
the cry of the mourning ones, the wicked will wail   835
before the visage of the eternal judge,
those who weakly believe in their works.
There will be revealed a greater terror
than ever was heard on earth from
the first creation. There it will be for each   840
of evildoers in that fast-approaching hour
much dearer than all this transitory creation,
that he might hide himself
in that victorious troop when the Lord of hosts,
the chief of nobles, will determine for all,   845
the loved and the hated, a reward according to right
for each of peoples. The need is great

þæt we gæstes wlite   ær þam gryre-brogan
on þas gæsnan tid   georne biþencen.
850 Nu is þon gelicost   swa we on lagu-flode
ofer cald wæter   ceolum liðan
geond sidne sæ,   sund-hengestum,
flod-wudu fergen.   Is þæt frecne stream
yða ofer-mæta   þe we her on lacað
855 geond þas wacan woruld,   windge holmas
ofer deop gelad.   Wæs se drohtað strong
ærþon we to londe   geliden hæfdon
ofer hreone hrycg.   Þa us help bicwom,
þæt us to hælo   hyþe gelædde,
860 Godes Gæst-Sunu,   ond us giefe sealde
þæt we oncnawan magun   ofer ceoles bord
hwær we sælan sceolon   sund-hengestas,
ealde yð-mearas,   ancrum fæste.
Utan us to þære hyðe   hyht staþelian,
865 ða us gerymde   rodera waldend,
halge on heahþu,   þa he to heofonum astag.

that before that terror in this barren hour
we should earnestly consider the state of our soul.
Now it is most like that we on the sea-flood   850
sail in ships over cold water
throughout the broad sea, in sea-steeds,
travel in wood-floaters. That stream is dangerous,
the waves without end that we toss on here
throughout this mutable world, windy the billows   855
over the deep waterway. The plight was hard
before we had sailed to land
over the rough ocean ridge. Then help came to us,
that led us to salvation in the harbor,
the spiritual Son of God, and gave us the gift   860
that we might know over the ship's side
where we must moor our sea-steeds,
the old wave-mares, fast with anchors.
Let us fix our hope in that harbor,
which for us the Ruler of the skies,   865
holy in the heights, opened when He ascended to heaven.

GUTHLAC B
The Death of St. Guthlac of Crowland

Ðæt is wide cuð   wera cneorissum,

820   folcum gefræge,   þætte frymþa God
       þone ærestan   ælda cynnes
       of þære clænestan,   cyning ælmihtig,
       foldan geworhte.   Ða wæs fruma niwe
       ęlda tudres,   onstæl wynlic,

825   fæger ond gefealic.   Fæder wæs acenned
       Adam ærest   þurh est Godes
       on neorxnawong,   þær him nænges wæs
       willan onsyn,   ne welan brosnung,
       ne lifes lyre   ne lices hryre,

830   ne dreames dryre   ne deaðes cyme,
       ac he on þam lande   lifgan moste
       ealra leahtra leas,   longe neotan
       niwra gefeana.   Þær he no þorfte
       lifes ne lissa   in þam leohtan ham

835   þurh ælda tid   ende gebidan,
       ac æfter fyrste   to þam færestan
       heofon-rices gefean   hweorfan mostan,
       leomu lic somud   ond lifes gæst,
       ond þær siþþan a   in sindreamum

840   to widan feore   wunian mostun
       Dryhtne on gesihðe,   butan deaðe forð,
       gif hy halges word   healdan woldun

That is widely known to generations,
celebrated among the people, that the God of origins,   820
the almighty king, made the first
of the human race from
the purest earth. It was the new beginning
of human offspring, a pleasant order,
fair and joyous. Our father Adam was born   825
first through the grace of God
in paradise, where for him there was no
lack of any desire, nor decay of prosperity,
nor loss of life, nor destruction of the body,
nor decline of gladness, nor the coming of death,   830
but he on that land could live
free of all faults to make use of
unheard of joys for a long time. There he did not need
to experience through old age an end of life
nor of favors in that bright home,   835
but he after an interval to the fairest
joy of the heavenly kingdom could turn,
limbs, body, and the soul of life together,
and there forever after in everlasting happiness
could always dwell   840
in the sight of the Lord without death,
if they would keep the word of the holy one

beorht in breostum,   ond his bebodu læstan,
æfnan on eðle.   Hy to ær aþreat
845 þæt hy waldendes   willan læsten,
ac his wif genom   wyrmes larum
blede forbodene,   ond of beame ahneop
wæstm biweredne   ofer word Godes,
wuldor-cyninges,   ond hyre were sealde
850 þurh deofles searo   deað-berende gyfl
þæt ða sinhiwan   to swylte geteah.
Siþþan se eþel   uðgenge wearð
Adame ond Euan,   eard-wica cyst
beorht oðbroden,   ond hyra bearnum swa,
855 eaferum æfter,   þa hy on uncyððu,
scomum scudende,   scofene wurdon
on gewin-woruld.   Weorces onguldon,
deopra firena,   þurh deaðes cwealm,
þe hy unsnyttrum   ær gefremedon.
860 Þære syn-wræce   siþþan sceoldon
mægð ond mæcgas   morþres ongyldon,
god-scyldge gyrn   þurh gæst-gedal,
deopra firena.   Deað in geþrong
fira cynne,   feond rixade
865 geond middan-geard.   Nænig monna wæs
of þam sige-tudre   siþþan æfre
Godes willan þæs georn,   ne gynn-wised,
þæt he bibugan mæge   þone bitran drync
þone Eue fyrn   Adame geaf,
870 byrelade bryd geong;   þæt him bam gescod

bright in their hearts and follow his bidding,
sustain it in their homeland. They tired too soon
of following the will of the ruler,   845
and his wife following the teachings of the snake took
the forbidden fruit and plucked from the tree
the protected plant against the word of God,
of the king of glory, and gave the death-bearing food
to her husband through the cunning of the devil   850
who thus lured the couple to their demise.
Afterward the homeland became alien
to Adam and Eve, the choicest of dwellings,
radiant, snatched away, and likewise for their children,
for their offspring after them, when they,   855
scurrying in shame, were thrust into an unknown land,
into a world of care. They paid through the plague of
death for the deed, the deep sins,
which they had foolishly committed earlier.
Ever since, men and women, guilty against God,   860
have had to pay dearly for mortal sin, for deep
transgressions, through the separation of the soul
[from the body] in that punishment for sins. Death
rushed upon mankind, the enemy ruled
throughout middle-earth. No one   865
from that victorious race was ever after
so ready in the will of God, nor knowledgeable,
that he could avoid the bitter drink
that Eve, the young bride, long ago
gave and served to Adam; that hurt them both   870

in þam deoran ham. Deað ricsade
ofer fold-buend, þeah þe fela wære
gæst-haligra, þær hi Godes willan
on mislicum monna gebihþum
875   æfter stede-wonga stowum fremedon;
sume ær, sume sið, sume in urra
æfter tæl-mearce tida gemyndum
sigor-lean sohtun. Us secgað bec
hu Guðlac wearð þurh Godes willan
880   eadig on Engle. He him ece geceas
meaht ond mund-byrd. Mære wurdon
his wundra geweorc wide ond side,
breme æfter burgum geond Bryten innan,
hu he monge oft þurh meaht Godes
885   gehælde hyge-geomre hefigra wita,
þe hine unsofte, adle gebundne,
sarge gesohtun of sið-wegum,
freorig-mode. Symle frofre þær
æt þam Godes cempan gearwe fundon,
890   helpe ond hælo. Nænig hæleþa is
þe areccan mæge oþþe rim wite
ealra þara wundra þe he in worulde her
þurh Dryhtnes giefe dugeþum gefremede.

II

Oft to þam wicum weorude cwomun
895   deofla deað-mægen duguþa byscyrede
hloþum þringan, þær se halga þeow
elnes an-hydig eard weardade.
Þær hy mislice mongum reordum
on þam westenne woðe hofun

in that dear home. Death ruled over the dwellers
of the earth, although there have been many
spiritually holy ones there doing God's will
in places, in various dwellings of humankind,
across the plains;   875
some before, some afterward, some of our own
at a date within memory of our times
sought the victory reward. Books tell us
how Guthlac through God's will became
blessed among the English. He chose for himself eternal   880
might and protection. His work of miracles
became renowned far and wide,
famous among the cities throughout Britain,
how he often, through the power of God,
healed many sorrowful ones of heavy pains,   885
who, bound by disease, sad in mind,
grieving severely, sought him
from distant ways. There they always readily found
comfort, help and healing,
from the warrior of God. No one   890
can relate or know the number
of all the miracles that he did for people
here in the world through the Lord's grace.

II

Often to those dwellings deadly bands of devils
separated from virtues came in hosts,   895
thronging in troops to where the holy servant,
resolute in courage, occupied his home.
There in many tongues
in that wilderness they raised diverse cries,

900 hludne here-cirm,   hiwes binotene,
 dreamum bidrorene.   Dryhtnes cempa,
 from folctoga,   feonda þreatum
 wiðstod stronglice.   Næs seo stund latu
 earmra gæsta,   ne þæt onbid long,
905 þæt þa wroht-smiðas   wop ahofun,
 hreopun hreðlease,   hleoþrum brugdon.
 Hwilum wedende   swa wilde deor
 cirmdon on corðre,   hwilum cyrdon eft
 minne man-sceaþan   on mennisc hiw
910 breahtma mæste,   hwilum brugdon eft
 awyrgde wærlogan   on wyrmes bleo,
 earme ad-loman   attre spiowdon.
 Symle hy Guðlac   gearene fundon,
 þonces gleawne.   He geþyldum bad,
915 þeah him feonda hloð   feorh-cwealm bude.
 Hwilum him to honda   hungre geþreatad
 fleag fugla cyn,   þær hy feorhnere
 witude fundon   ond hine weorðedon
 meaglum stefnum.   Hwilum mennisce
920 aras eaðmedum   eft neosedon,
 ond þær sið-frome   on þam sige-wonge
 æt þam halgan þeowon   helpe gemetton,
 ferðþes frofre.   Nænig forþum wæs,
 þæt he æwisc-mod   eft siðade,
925 hean, hyhta leas,   ac se halga wer
 ælda gehwylces   þurh þa æþelan meaht,
 þe hine seoslige   sohtun on ðearfe,

a loud war-shout, deprived of form,   900
bereft of joys. The Lord's warrior,
the bold captain, strongly withstood
the troops of enemies. The hour
of the wretched spirits was not late nor the waiting long
until the strife-workers raised up weeping,   905
the inglorious ones cried out, varied their sounds.
Sometimes raving like wild animals they shrieked
together with the greatest tumult, sometimes they
turned again, the vile evil foes, into human shape
sometimes the cursed promise-breakers   910
changed again into the form of a dragon,
and the miserable fire-maimed wretches would spew
venom. They always found Guthlac ready,
wise in thought. He endured patiently,
although the band of enemies threatened his life.   915
Sometimes, impelled by hunger,
a species of birds flew to his hands, where they found
assured nourishment and honored him
with earnest voices. Sometimes human
messengers humbly visited him,   920
and there those eager to be going on the victory plain
found help, comfort for the heart,
from the holy servant. Indeed, no one
turned back ashamed,
downcast, bereft of hope, but the holy man   925
through his noble power healed both body and soul
of each person, sorrowful people, who,

hæleð hyge-geomre,   hælde bu tu
lic ond sawle,   þenden lifes weard,
930   ece ælmihtig,   unnan wolde
þæt he blædes her   brucan moste,
worulde lifes.   Wæs gewinnes þa
yrmþa for eorðan   ende-dogor
þurh nyd-gedal   neah geþrungen,
935   siþþan he on westenne   wic-eard geceas,
fiftynu gear,   þa wæs frofre Gæst
eadgum æ-bodan   ufan onsended,
halig of heahþu.   Hreþer innan born,
afysed on forð-sið.   Him færinga
940   adl in gewod.   He on elne swa þeah
ungeblyged bad   beorhtra gehata
bliþe in burgum.   Wæs þam ban-cofan
æfter niht-glome   neah geþrungen,
breost-hord onboren.   Wæs se bliþa gæst
945   fus on forð-weg.   Nolde Fæder engla
in þisse won-sælgan   worulde life
leahtra leasne   long-fyrst ofer þæt
wunian leton,   þe him on weorcum her
on his dagena tid   dædum gecwemde
950   elne unslawe.   Ða se ælmihtiga
let his hond cuman   þær se halga þeow,
deor-mod on degle   dom-eadig bad,
heard ond hyge-rof.   Hyht wæs geniwad,
blis in breostum.   Wæs se ban-cofa
955   adle onæled,   in-bendum fæst,
lic-hord onlocen.   Leomu hefegedon,
sarum gesohte.   He þæt soð gecneow

afflicted, sought him in need,
when the guardian of life,
eternal and almighty, wanted to let   930
them enjoy glory here,
life in the world. Then had the final day of strife,
of miseries on account of the world,
through forced separation pressed near,
since he had chosen a dwelling place in the wilderness   935
fifteen years before when the consoling Spirit,
holy from the heights, was sent from above,
to the blessed preacher. His heart burned within,
impelled on the onward journey. Sickness had suddenly
entered him. In courage nevertheless he   940
awaited undismayed the bright promises
happy in the dwellings. The bone-dwelling was
closely oppressed in the gloom of night,
his breast-hoard weakened. The joyful spirit was eager
for the path onward. The Father of angels did not want   945
to let the one free from sins dwell in this unhappy
life of the world for a long time after that,
he who through works
during his days here pleased him with his deeds,
with quick courage. Then the almighty   950
let his hand come where the holy servant,
bold-minded in the darkness, blessed with power, waited,
hard and stout of mind. Hope was renewed,
joy in the breast. The bone-dwelling was
consumed by sickness, fast with inner chains,   955
the body was unlocked. His limbs grew heavy,
attacked by pains. He knew that

43

þæt hine ælmihtig   ufan neosade,
meotud fore miltsum.   He his mod-sefan
960 wið þam fær-hagan   fæste trymede
feonda gewinna.   Næs he forht seþeah,
ne seo adl-þracu   egle on mode,
ne deað-gedal,   ac him Dryhtnes lof
born in breostum,   brond-hat lufu
965 sigorfæst in sefan,   seo him sara gehwylc
symle forswiðde.   Næs him sorg-cearu
on þas lænan tid,   þeah his lic ond gæst
hyra somwiste,   sinhiwan tu,
deore gedælden.   Dagas forð scridun,
970 niht-helma genipu.   Wæs neah seo tid
þæt he fyrn-gewyrht   fyllan sceolde
þurh deaðes cyme,   domes hleotan,
efne þæs ilcan   þe usse yldran fyrn
frecne onfengon,   swa him biforan worhton
975 þa ærestan   ælda cynnes.

III

Ða wæs Guðlace   on þa geocran tid
mægen gemeðgad,   mod swiþe heard,
elnes an-hydig.   Wæs seo adl þearl,
hat ond heoro-grim.   Hreþer innan weol,
980 born ban-loca.   Bryþen wæs ongunnen
þætte Adame   Eue gebyrmde
æt fruman worulde.   Feond byrlade
ærest þære idese,   ond heo Adame,
hyre swæsum were,   siþþan scencte
985 bittor bæde-weg.   Þæs þa byre siþþan
grimme onguldon   gaful-rædenne
þurh ær-gewyrht,   þætte ænig ne wæs

44

the almighty, the measurer, visited him
from above out of mercy. He firmly fixed
his heart against the sudden onslaught   960
of enemy attacks. Still, he was not afraid,
nor was the force of the disease hateful in his mind,
nor the death-separation, but the praise of the Lord
burned in his breast, ardent love
victory-firm in his heart, which always overcame   965
each of his pains. There was no sorrowful anxiety in him
about this transitory time, although his body and spirit,
the wedded pair, would separate their dear
life together. The days passed on,
the darkness of the cover of night. The time was near   970
when he must fulfill the ancient decree
through the coming of death, obtain judgment,
even the same that our elders long ago
horribly received, as before them the first
of the human race did.   975

III

Then for Guthlac in that grievous time
his strength was exhausted, his mind very hard,
resolute in courage. The sickness was severe,
hot and battle-grim. His breast surged within,
his bone-coffer burned. The brew had begun   980
that Eve fermented for Adam
at the beginning of the world. The enemy poured it out
first to the woman, and to Adam,
to her dear husband, she then offered
the bitter drinking cup. Their descendants then   985
paid terrible tribute
on account of the ancient deed so that not one

fyra cynnes   from fruman siððan
mon on moldan,   þætte meahte him
990   gebeorgan ond bibugan   þone bleatan drync,
deopan deað-weges,   ac him duru sylfa
on þa sliðnan tid   sona ontyneð,
in-gong geopenað.   Ne mæg ænig þam
flæsce bifongen   feore wiðstondan,
995   ricra ne heanra,   ac hine ræseð on
gifrum grapum.   Swa wæs Guðlace
enge anhoga   ætryhte þa
æfter niht-scuan   neah geþyded,
wiga wæl-gifre.   Hine wunade mid
1000   an ombeht-þegn,   se hine æghwylce
daga neosade.   Ongan ða deop-hydig,
gleaw-mod gongan   to Godes temple,
þær he eþel-bodan   inne wiste,
þone leofestan   lareow gecorenne,
1005   ond þa in eode   eadgum to spræce,
wolde hyrcnigan   halges lara,
mildes meþel-cwida.   Fonde þa his mon-dryhten
adl-werigne;   him ðæt in gefeol
hefig æt heortan.   Hyge-sorge wæg,
1010   micle mod-ceare.   Ongan ða his magu frignan:
"Hu gewearð þe þus,   wine-dryhten min,
fæder, freonda hleo,   ferð gebysgad,
nearwe genæged?   Ic næfre þe,
þeoden leofesta,   þyslicne ær
1015   gemette þus meðne.   Meaht þu meðel-cwidum
worda gewealdan?   Is me on wene geþuht,
þæt þe untrymnes   adle gongum
on þisse nyhstan   niht bysgade,

of the human race from the beginning on,
not anyone on earth, could
find protection and avoid the wretched drink,   990
the deep cup of death, but instead at that cruel time
one immediately opens the door for one's self,
the entrance opens. No one
enveloped in flesh can resist it with life,
neither the high nor the low, but it rushes on you   995
with greedy clutches. So the cruel solitary one,
the warrior greedy for slaughter,
came close, right up to Guthlac,
through the shade of night. A servant stayed
with him, visited him   1000
every day. Deep-thoughted, wise,
he went to God's temple,
where he knew the land's preacher,
the dearest, chosen teacher, was inside
and then entered to talk with the blessed one;   1005
he wanted to hear the holy one's teachings,
the gentle one's discourses. Then he found his master
exhausted with the disease; that struck him heavy
at heart. He felt anxiety,
great grief. Then his servant asked: 1010
"How did you come to this, my friendly lord,
father, protector of friends, afflicted at heart,
closely assailed? Never before,
dearest prince, have I found
you so weary. Can you control your words   1015
in conversation? Is seems likely to me
that infirmity, through the disease's attack,
afflicted you last night, seized

sar-bennum gesoht.   Þæt me sorgna is
1020 hatost on hreþre,   ær þu hyge minne
ferð afrefre.   Wast þu, freo-dryhten,
hu þeos adle scyle   ende gesettan?"
Him þa sið oncwæð,   sona ne meahte
oroð up geteon;   wæs him in bogen
1025 bittor ban-coþa.   Beald reordade
eadig on elne,   ondcwis ageaf:
"Ic wille secgan   þæt me sar gehran,
wærc in gewod   in ðisse wonnan niht,
lic-hord onleac.   Leomu hefegiað,
1030 sarum gesohte.   Sceal þis sawel-hus,
fæge flæsc-homa,   fold-ærne biþeaht,
leomu, lames geþacan,   leger-bedde fæst
wunian wæl-ræste.   Wiga nealæceð,
unlæt laces.   Ne bið þæs lengra swice
1035 sawel-gedales   þonne seofon-niht
fyrst-gemearces,   þæt min feorh heonan
on þisse eahteþan   ende geseceð
dæg scriþende.   Þonne dogor beoð
on mold-wege   min forð scriþen,
1040 sorg gesweðrad,   ond ic siþþan mot
fore meotudes cneowum   meorda hleotan,
gingra geafena,   ond Godes lomber
in sindreamum   siþþan awo
forð folgian;   is nu fus ðider
1045 gæst siþes georn.   Nu þu gearwe const
leoma lif-gedal;   long is þis onbid
worulde lifes."   Ða wæs wop ond heaf,
geongum geocor sefa,   geomrende hyge,

48

you with painful wounds. The
hottest of sorrows will be in my heart until you   1020
can comfort my mind, my spirit. Do you know,
noble lord, how this disease will end?"
After a pause he answered him because he couldn't
catch his breath right away; the bitter, pernicious disease
had sunk in him. Brave, blessed in courage,   1025
he spoke and gave answer:
"I want to say that pain seized me, suffering
entered in during this dark night, unlocked
the body hoard. My limbs grow heavy,
seized with pains. This soul-house, the   1030
fated fleshly home, must be covered with an earth-house,
the limbs, the clay wrappings, fast in the bed of sickness,
must remain in the deathbed. The warrior
approaches, ready for the struggle. The delay
until soul parts from body will last no longer   1035
than seven nights, so
that my spirit will find its end
on this eighth day passing. Then my days
on the earth-way will be passed, sorrow stilled,
and before the knees of the creator   1040
I can afterward share in rewards, in new gifts, and
always follow the lamb of God
in eternal joys; now the spirit,
eager for the journey, is ready.
Now you clearly know the   1045
parting from life of the limbs; long is this waiting
in the world of life." Then was weeping and mourning,
the heart was sad in the young man, his mind in grief,

siþþan he gehyrde   þæt se halga wæs
1050   forð-siþes fus.   He þæs fær-spelles
fore his mon-dryhtne   mod-sorge wæg,
hefige æt heortan;   hreþer innan swearc,
hyge hreow-cearig,   þæs þe his hlaford geseah
ellor-fusne.   He þæs onbæru
1055   habban ne meahte,   ac he hate let
torn þoliende   tearas geotan,
weallan wæg-dropan.   Wyrd ne meahte
in fægum leng   feorg gehealdan,
deore frætwe,   þonne him gedemed wæs.

IV

1060   Ongeat gæsta halig   geomor-modes
drusendne hyge.   Ongan þa duguþa hleo,
glæd-mod Gode leof,   geongran retan,
wine leofestan   wordum negan:
"Ne beo þu unrot,   ðeah þeos adl me
1065   innan æle.   Nis me earfeðe
to geþolianne   þeodnes willan,
dryhtnes mines,   ne ic þæs deaðes hafu
on þas seocnan tid   sorge on mode,
ne ic me here-hloðe   helle þegna
1070   swiðe onsitte,   ne mæg synne on me
facnes frum-bearn   fyrene gestælan,
lices leahtor,   ac in lige sceolon
sorg-wylmum soden   sar wanian,
wræc-sið wepan,   wilna biscirede
1075   in þam deað-sele   duguða gehwylcre,

once he heard that the holy man was ready
for the onward journey. Because of that dreadful news,   1050
he felt distress, was heavy in heart, for his master;
his breast grew dark,
his mind troubled, because he saw his lord
ready to depart elsewhere. He could not keep his
composure over it, but suffering grief, he let   1055
the burning tears pour out,
the drops of water surge. The course of events could not
hold the life, the dear treasure, longer
in one doomed to death than was ordained for him.

IV

The holy one of souls perceived the drooping spirit   1060
of the sorrowful one. The protector of men,
joyful in mind, dear to God, then began cheering up the
younger man, to address in words his dearest friend:
"Don't be sad, although this disease
burns inside me. It is no burden for me   1065
to bear the will of the prince,
of my lord, nor do I have sorrow in my heart
because of death in this time of sickness,
nor do I greatly fear the hostile troop of attendants
from hell, nor may the firstborn of   1070
evil accuse me of sin, of wickedness, crime
of the body, but in the flame, afflicted with
waves of sorrow, they must bewail their pain,
lament the exile-journey, stripped in the death-hall
of desires, of each glory,   1075

lufena ond lissa.   Min þæt leofe bearn,
ne beo þu on sefan to seoc.   Ic eom siþes fus
up-eard niman,   edleana georn
in þam ecan gefean,   ær-gewyrhtum
1080   geseon sigora Frean,   min þæt swæse bearn.
Nis me wracu ne gewin,   þæt ic wuldres God
sece swegel-cyning,   þær is sib ond blis,
domfæstra dream,   Dryhten ondweard,
þam ic georne   gæst-gerynum,
1085   in þas dreorgan tid   dædum cwemde,
mode ond mægne.   Ic þa meorde wat
leahtorlease,   lean unhwilen,
halig on heahþu.   Þær min hyht myneð
to gesecenne,   sawul fundað
1090   of lic-fate   to þam longan gefean
in ead-welan.   Nis þes eþel me
ne sar ne sorg.   Ic me sylfum wat
æfter lices hryre   lean unhwilen.”
Ða se wuldor-maga   worda gestilde,
1095   rof run-wita;   wæs him ræste neod,
reonig-modum.   Rodor swamode
ofer niðða bearn,   niht-rim scridon,
deorc ofer dugeðum.   Þa se dæg bicwom
on þam se lifgenda   in lic-homan,
1100   ece ælmihtig   ærist gefremede,
Dryhten mid dreame,   ða he of deaðe aras
onwald of eorðan   in þa eastor-tid,
ealra þrymma þrym,   ðreata mæstne
to heofonum ahof,   ða he from helle astag.
1105   Swa se eadga wer   in þa æþelan tid

of hopes and mercies. My dear child,
don't be sick at heart. I am ready for the journey,
eager to take up abode in the dwelling of rewards on high
in that eternal joy, to see the Lord of victories
for deeds of old, my beloved child.   1080
It is not a hardship or strife for me that I seek the God of
glory, the heavenly king, where peace and bliss
are, the joy of the faithful, the present Lord,
whom with spiritual mysteries
in this sad time I eagerly pleased with deeds   1085
in heart and in strength. I know that flawless reward,
eternal requital,
holy in the heights. There my hope is impelled
to visit, the soul struggles
from the body to that long joy   1090
in blessedness. This home has neither
pain nor sorrow for me. I know that
eternal award awaits me after the fall of the body."
Then the glorious man, the brave sage,
fell silent; weary in spirit,   1095
he had to rest. The firmament moved
over the sons of men; a number of nights glided by,
dark over the troops. Then the day came
on which the living one, eternal and
almighty, brought about a resurrection of the body,   1100
the Lord with joy when he rose from death
powerful from earth in the Easter time,
glory of all glories, raised to the heavens
the greatest of hosts, when he ascended from hell.
So the blessed man rejoicing in bliss,   1105

on þone beorhtan dæg   blissum hremig,
milde ond gemetfæst,   mægen unsofte
elne geæfnde.   Aras ða eorla wynn,
heard hyge-snottor,   swa he hraþost meahte,
meðe for ðam miclan bysgum.   Ongon þa his mod
                                                        staþelian
leohte geleafan,   lac onsægde
deop-hycgende   dryhtne to willan
gæst-gerynum   in Godes temple,
ond his þegne ongon,   swa þam þeodne geras,
þurh gæstes giefe   godspel bodian,
secgan sigor-tacnum,   ond his sefan trymman
wundrum to wuldre   in þa wlitigan gesceaft
to ead-welan,   swa he ær ne sið
æfre to ealdre   oðre swylce
on þas lænan tid   lare gehyrde,
ne swa deoplice   dryhtnes geryne
þurh menniscne   muð areccan
on sidum sefan.   Him wæs soþra geþuht
þæt hit ufancundes   engles wære
of swegl-dreamum,   swiþor micle
mægen-þegnes word,   þonne æniges monnes lar,
wera ofer eorðan.   Him þæt wundra mæst
gesewen þuhte,   þæt swylc snyttru-cræft
ænges hæleða her   hreþer weardade,
dryhta bearna,   wæs þæs deoplic eall

mild and modest on the bright day,
performed with difficulty, with courage, a feat of strength
in that noble time. The joy of men rose then,
hard, wise in mind, as soon as he could, weary
from the great afflictions. He then began to fix his mind   1110
on the heavenly faith, made an offering
according to the lord's wish, deeply pondering
the spiritual mysteries in the temple of God,
and began, as befitted the master,
to preach the gospel through grace of spirit, to relate   1115
to his attendant the signs of victory and to fortify
his mind wondrously as to the glory, the blessedness
in that beautiful creation in such a way as he neither
before nor after ever in his life heard other such teaching
in this transitory time,   1120
nor the human mouth relate so deeply
the secret of the lord
in extensive understanding. It seemed to him more
truthful that it was from the heavenly joys
of a celestial angel, much more the word   1125
of a mighty attendant than the teaching of any man,
of the peoples throughout the earth. To him what he
    beheld
seemed the greatest of wonders that such wisdom
dwelled in the breast of any warrior here,
of any of human offspring, so profound was all   1130

word ond wisdom,   ond þæs weres stihtung,
mod ond mægen-cræft,   þe him meotud engla,
gæsta geocend   forgiefen hæfde.

v

Wæron feowere ða   forð gewitene
1135   dagas on rime,   þæs se dryhtnes þegn
on elne bad,   adle gebysgad,
sarum geswenced.   Ne he sorge wæg
geocorne sefan   gæst-gedales,
dreorigne hyge.   Deað nealæcte,
1140   stop stal-gongum,   strong ond hreðe
sohte sawel-hus.   Com se seofeða dæg
ældum ondweard,   þæs þe him in gesonc,
hat, heortan neah,   hilde-scurum
flacor flan-þracu,   feorh-hord onleac,
1145   searo-cægum gesoht.   Ongon ða snottor hæle,
ar, onbeht-þegn,   æþeles neosan
to þam halgan hofe,   fond þa hlingendne
fusne on forð-siþ   frean unwenne,
gæst-haligne   in Godes temple
1150   soden sar-wylmum.   Wæs þa sihste tid
on midne dæg,   wæs his mon-dryhtne
ende-dogor   ætryhte þa.
Nearwum genæged   nyd-costingum,
awrecen wæl-pilum,   wlo ne meahte
1155   oroð up geteon,   ellen-spræce
hleoþor ahebban.   Ongon ða hyge-geomor,
freorig ond ferð-werig,   fusne gretan,

the man's word and wisdom and direction,
the mind and mighty power that the creator of angels,
the preserver of souls, had granted him.

v

Then four days had passed
while the servant of the lord,   1135
afflicted by disease, troubled by pains,
endured in courage. He did not feel sorrow
or have a grievous heart, a mournful mind, over the
separation of the soul from the body. Death drew near,
advanced with stealthy steps, strong and savage   1140
sought the soul-house. The seventh day came
to mankind since hot, near to the heart,
a battle shower, a flickering force of arrows,
sank into him, unlocked the life-hoard,
sought it with treacherous keys. The wise man,   1145
the servant, the attendant, began to seek the noble one
in that holy house, where he found his hopeless lord,
the holy-spirited one, leaning in god's temple,
ready for the onward journey,
afflicted with surges of pain. It was the sixth hour   1150
at midday; for his master
the final day was at hand.
Assailed hard by painful trials,
pierced by deadly darts, he indeed could not
take a breath, raise a sound in   1155
brave speech. He began then, sad in mind,
chilled and with a weary heart, to greet the eagerly
        departing,

meðne mod-glædne,   bæd hine þurh mihta scyppend,
gif he his word-cwida   wealdan meahte,
1160 spræce ahebban,   þæt him on spellum gecyðde,
onwrige worda gongum,   hu he his wisna truwade,
drohtes on ðære dimman adle,   ær ðon hine deað
                                                        onsægde.

Him se eadga wer   ageaf ondsware,
leof mon leofum,   þeah he late meahte,
1165 eorl ellen-heard,   oreþe gebredan:
"Min þæt swæse bearn,   nis nu swiþe feor
þam ytemestan   ende-dogor
nyd-gedales,   þæt ðu þa nyhstan scealt
in woruld-life   worda minra,
1170 næfre leana biloren,   lare gehyran,
noht longe ofer þis.   Læst ealle well
wære ond winescype,   word þa wit spræcon,
leofast manna."   "Næfre ic lufan sibbe,
þeoden, æt þearfe   þine forlæte
1175 asanian!"   "Beo þu on sið gearu,
siþþan lic ond leomu   ond þes lifes gæst
asundrien   somwist hyra
þurh feorg-gedal.   Fyr æfter þon
þæt þu gesecge   sweostor minre,
1180 þære leofestan,   on longne weg
to þam fægran gefean   forð-sið minne,

tired, glad-spirited man, asked him by the creator of
powers, if he could wield words, raise speech
so that he would make known in conversations,   1160
reveal in a stream of words, how he might trust his ways,
    his manner
of life in that wretched sickness, before death should
make sacrifice of him. The blessed man gave answer,
the beloved one to the beloved, although the courageous
man could barely draw breath: 1165
"My dear child, it isn't too far now
to the very last day
of the forced dissolution, so that not long after this you
must hear the teaching in this worldly life
of the last of my words, which are   1170
never lacking in benefits. Carry out well all the promise
and friendship, the words we two have spoken,
dearest of men." "Never will I let the peace of love,
master, grow weak in your time
of need!" "Be ready for a journey,   1175
after my body and limbs and the spirit of life
sever their life together
through death. Go now
so you can tell my sister,
that most beloved one, about my journey forth   1180
on the long path to that fair joy

on ecne eard,   ond hyre eac gecyð
wordum minum,   þæt ic me warnade
hyre onsyne   ealle þrage
1185 in woruld-life,   for ðy ic wilnode
þæt wit unc eft   in þam ecan gefean
on swegl-wuldre   geseon mostun
fore onsyne   eces deman
leahtra lease.   Þær sceal lufu uncer
1190 wærfæst wunian,   þær wit wilna a
in ðære beorhtan byrig   brucan motun,
eades mid englum.   Ðu hyre eac saga
þæt heo þis ban-fæt   beorge bifæste,
lame biluce,   lic orsawle
1195 in þeostor-cofan,   þær hit þrage sceal
in sond-hofe   siþþan wunian."
Ða wearð mod-geþanc   miclum gebisgad,
þream forþrycced,   þurh þæs þeodnes word,
ombeht-þegne,   þa he ædre oncneow
1200 frean feorh-gedal,   þæt hit feor ne wæs,
ende-dogor.   Ongon þa ofostlice
to his wine-dryhtne   wordum mæðlan:
"Ic þec halsige,   hæleþa leofost
gumena cynnes,   þurh gæsta weard,
1205 þæt þu hyge-sorge   heortan minre
geeþe, eorla wyn.   Nis þe ende feor,
þæs þe ic on galdrum   ongieten hæbbe.
Oft mec geomor sefa   gehþa gemanode,
hat æt heortan,   hyge gnornende
1210 nihtes nearwe,   ond ic næfre þe,
fæder, frofor min,   frignan dorste.
Symle ic gehyrde,   þonne heofones gim,

60

in the eternal dwelling, and make known to her, too,
in my words that I denied myself
her face all the time
in worldly life because I wanted   1185
us to see each other again,
free from sins, in that eternal joy
in heavenly glory before the face
of the eternal judge. There our love shall
remain steadfast where always   1190
in that bright city we may enjoy our desires,
bliss among the angels. Say to her also
that she should commit this corpse to a mound,
lock in clay the soulless body
in the dark chamber, where it must   1195
afterward for a time abide in the sand-dwelling."
Then the servant's mind became greatly
afflicted, cruelly overwhelmed,
at the master's word, when he clearly knew
his lord's death, that it was not far off,   1200
his final day. He began then hastily
to speak these words to his friend and master:
"I beseech you by the guardian of spirits,
dearest of heroes among the human race,
joy of mankind, that you might alleviate the   1205
sorrow of my heart. The end is not far,
as I have understood by your divinations.
Often my sad soul, hot at heart,
my mourning mind, reminded me of cares
closely at night, and I never dared, father,   1210
my solace, to ask you.
Always when the jewel of heaven,

61

wyn-condel wera,   west onhylde,
swegl-beorht sunne   setl-gonges fus
1215   on æfen-tid,   oþerne mid þec,
þegn æt geþeahte.   Ic þæs þeodnes word,
ares uncuþes   oft neosendes,
dæg-woman bitweon   ond þære deorcan niht,
meþel-cwide mæcges,   ond on morgne swa,
1220   ongeat geomor-mod,   gæstes spræce,
gleawes in geardum.   Huru, ic giet ne wat,
ær þu me, frea min,   furþor cyðe
þurh cwide þinne,   hwonan his cyme sindon."

VI

Ða se eadga wer   ageaf ondsware
1225   leofum æfter longre hwile,   swa he late meahte,
elnes oncyðig,   oreþe gewealdan:
"Hwæt, þu me, wine min,   wordum nægest,
fusne frignest,   þæs þe ic furþum ær
æfre on ealdre   ængum ne wolde
1230   monna ofer moldan   melda weorðan,
þegne on þeode,   butan þe nuða,
þy læs þæt wundredan   weras ond idesa,
ond on geað gutan,   gieddum mænden
bi me lifgendum.   Huru, ic nolde sylf
1235   þurh gielp-cwide   gæstes mines
frofre gelettan,   ne Fæder mines
æfre geæfnan,   æbylg Godes.
Symle me onsende   Sige-Dryhten min,
folca feorh-giefa,   siþþan ic furþum ongon
1240   on þone æfteran   anseld bugan

the joyous candle of mankind,
the heaven-bright sun eager for setting in the evening
reclined in the west, I heard another person with you,   1215
an attendant in consultation. Sad at heart, I heard the
    words of the master,
the discourse of the man, the speech of the spirit,
of the wise one in the yards,
of the unknown messenger visiting
often between dawn and the dark of night,   1220
and in the morning, too. Yet I still will not know
until you, my lord, through your speech
further explain to me where he comes from."

VI

Then after a long time the blessed man
gave answer to the dear one slowly,   1225
revealing courage, controlling his breath as best he could:
"How much, my friend, you address me in words,
question me ready to depart, about what I never before
in my life wanted to tell to anyone
on earth, to any attendant   1230
among the people, except to you now,
lest men and women should have marveled at that
and have poured out mockery, complained about me in
songs my whole life. Indeed, I did not want
to hinder my soul's consolation   1235
through boasting, nor ever
cause my Father's, God's, wrath.
My victorious Lord, the life-giver of the people,
since I first began
the second year of my inhabiting   1240

63

gear-gemearces,   gæst haligne,
engel ufancundne,   se mec efna gehwam,
meahtig meotudes þegn,   ond on morgne eft,
sigorfæst gesohte,   ond me sara gehwylc
1245　gehælde hyge-sorge,   ond me in hreþre bileac
wuldres wil-boda   wisdomes giefe
micle monigfealdran   þonne ænig mon wite
in life her,   þe me alyfed nis
to gecyþenne   cwicra ængum
1250　on fold-wege   fira cynnes,
þæt me ne meahte   monna ænig
bideaglian   hwæt he dearninga
on hyge hogde   heortan geþoncum,
siþþan he me fore eagum   onsyne wearð.
1255　A ic on mode mað   monna gehwylcne
þeodnes þrym-cyme   oð þisne dæg.
Leofast monna,   nu ic for lufan þinre,
ond geferscype   þæt wit fyrn mid unc
longe læstan,   nelle ic lætan þe
1260　æfre unrotne   æfter ealdorlege
meðne mod-seocne   minre geweorðan,
soden sorg-wælmum.   A ic sibbe wiþ þe
healdan wille.   Nu of hreþer-locan
to þam soþan gefean   sawel fundað.
1265　Nis seo tid latu,   tydrað þis ban-fæt,
greot-hord gnornað,   gæst hine fyseð
on ecne geard,   ut-siþes georn
on sellan gesetu.   Nu ic swiðe eom

the hermitage has always sent me a holy spirit, a celestial
angel, who visited every evening, the mighty attendant
of the measurer, and in the morning, too,
firm in victory, and healed each of my pains,
my anxiety of mind, and in my heart the glorious   1245
messenger of joy locked the gift of wisdom
much more manifold than any one in this life
may know and which it is not
granted me to reveal to anyone
living on earth,   1250
that no one may hide
from me what he secretly
should ponder in the thoughts of his heart,
when he was visible before my eyes.
I have always hidden inside my mind   1255
the glorious coming of the master from everybody until
today. Dearest of men, now for love of you
and the brotherhood that we two in the past
long shared, I will not let you
ever become sad after my death,   1260
weary, sick at heart,
disturbed with waves of sorrow. I will always hold
friendship with you. Now from my breast
my soul strives after the true joy.
Time is not sluggish, this body grows weak,   1265
the earthen-hoard mourns, the spirit hastens
into the eternal dwelling-place, eager for the departure
to better habitations. I am now greatly

weorce gewergad." Ða to þam wage gesag,
1270 heafelan onhylde, hyrde þa gena
ellen on innan. Oroð stundum teah
mægne modig; him of muðe cwom
swecca swetast. Swylce on sumeres tid
stincað on stowum staþelum fæste
1275 wynnum æfter wongum wyrta geblowene,
hunig-flowende, swa þæs halgan wæs
ondlongne dæg oþ æfen forð
oroð up hlæden. Þa se æþela glæm
setl-gong sohte, swearc norð-rodor
1280 won under wolcnum, woruld miste oferteah,
þystrum biþeahte, þrong niht ofer tiht
londes frætwa. Ða cwom leohta mæst,
halig of heofonum hædre scinan,
beorhte ofer burg-salu. Bad se þe sceolde
1285 eadig on elne ende-dogor,
awrecen wæl-strælum. Wuldres scima,
æþele ymb æþelne, ondlonge niht
scan scir-wered. Scadu sweþredon,
tolysed under lyfte. Wæs se leohta glæm
1290 ymb þæt halge hus, heofonlic condel,
from æfen-glome oþþæt eastan cwom
ofer deop gelad dægred-woma,
weder-tacen wearm. Aras se wuldor-mago,
eadig elnes gemyndig, spræc to his onbeht-þegne,

wearied by effort." Then he sank down by the wall,
bowed his head, yet still made hard   1270
the courage within him. At times he drew breath
brave in strength; from his mouth came
the sweetest of scents. As in the summer time
blossoming plants in some places, flowing with honey,
held fast by their roots, smell pleasantly   1275
along the plains, so was the breath of the holy one
drawn up all day long until evening.
Then the noble radiance
sought its setting, the northern sky grew dark,
dusky under the clouds, covered the world with mist,   1280
enveloped it with darkness, night forced itself over the
expanse of the land's adornments. Then the greatest
of lights came, holy from the heavens clearly shining,
bright over the houses. He awaited his final day,
he who had to, blessed in courage,   1285
pierced with fatal arrows. The splendor of glory,
noble around the noble one, shone bright
the whole night. The shadows abated,
loosened under the heavens. The bright radiance,
the heavenly candle, surrounded that holy house   1290
from twilight until break of day,
the sign of warm weather came from the east
over the deep path. The glorious man arose,
the blessed one mindful of courage spoke to his servant,

1295 torht to his treowum gesiþe: "Tid is þæt þu fere,
ond þa ærendu   eal biþence,
ofestum læde,   swa ic þe ær bibead,
lac to leofre.   Nu of lice is,
god-dreama georn,   gæst swiðe fus."

1300 Ahof þa his honda,   husle gereorded,
eað-mod þy æþelan gyfle,   swylce he his eagan ontynde,
halge heafdes gimmas,   biseah þa to heofona rice,
glæd-mod to geofona leanum,   ond þa his gæst onsende
weorcum wlitigne   in wuldres dream.

VII

1305 Ða wæs Guðlaces   gæst gelæded
eadig on up-weg.   Englas feredun
to þam longan gefean,   lic colode,
belifd under lyfte.   Ða þær leoht ascan,
beama beorhtast.   Eal þæt beacen wæs

1310 ymb þæt halge hus,   heofonlic leoma,
from foldan up   swylce fyren tor
ryht aræred   oð rodera hrof,
gesewen under swegle,   sunnan beorhtra,
æþel-tungla wlite.   Engla þreatas

1315 sige-leoð sungon,   sweg wæs on lyfte
gehyred under heofonum,   haligra dream.
Swa se burg-stede wæs   blissum gefylled,
swetum stencum   ond swegl-wundrum,
eadges yrfe-stol,   engla hleoðres,

1320 eal innanweard.   Þær wæs ænlicra

the beautiful one to his faithful companion: "It's time for   1295
you to go and see to all the errands, quickly
take the gift, as I earlier asked you,
to the beloved. Now from the body, eager for the joys
of God, my spirit is very ready to depart."
Then he, the humble one, raised his hands, refreshed by   1300
    the Eucharist,
by that noble food; likewise joyful in mind he opened his
eyes, the head's holy jewels, then looked to the kingdom
of heaven, to the rewards of grace and sent his spirit
made beautiful by his deeds into the joy of glory.

VII

The spirit of Guthlac was then led   1305
blessed on the upward path. Angels brought it
to that long joy, the body grew cold,
deprived of life under the sky. Then a light shone there,
the brightest of beams. That beacon, the heavenly light,
surrounded that holy house,   1310
rose up from the earth like a fiery tower
rightly raised to the roof of the firmament
visible under the sky, brighter than the sun,
than the beauty of the noble stars. Throngs of angels
sang a song of victory; the sound in the air was   1315
heard under the heavens, the joy of the holy.
Thus the citadel, the seat of the blessed one,
was filled entirely within with the exultation,
with sweet smells and heavenly wonders of angels.
There it was more excellent   1320

ond wynsumra   þonne hit in worulde mæge
stefn areccan,   hu se stenc ond se sweg,
heofonlic hleoþor   ond se halga song,
gehyred wæs,   heah-þrym Godes,
1325   breahtem æfter breahtme.   Beofode þæt ealond,
fold-wong onþrong.   Ða afyrhted wearð
ar, elnes biloren,   gewat þa ofestlice
beorn unhyðig,   þæt he bat gestag,
wæg-hengest wræc,   wæter-þisa for,
1330   snel under sorgum.   Swegl hate scan,
blac ofer burg-salo.   Brim-wudu scynde,
leoht, lade fus.   Lagu-mearg snyrede,
gehlæsted to hyðe,   þæt se hærn-flota
æfter sund-plegan   sond-lond gespearn,
1335   grond wið greote.   Gnorn-sorge wæg
hate æt heortan,   hyge geomurne,
meðne mod-sefan,   se þe his mondryhten,
life bilidene,   last weardian
wiste, wine leofne.   Him þæs wopes hring
1340   torne gemonade.   Teagor yðum weol,
hate hleor-dropan,   ond on hreþre wæg
micle mod-ceare.   He þære mægeð sceolde
lace gelædan   lað-spel to soð.
Cwom þa freorig-ferð   þær seo fæmne wæs,
1345   wuldres wyn-mæg.   He þa wyrd ne mað,
fæges forð-sið.   Fus-leoð agol

70

and more pleasant than a worldly voice
could relate, how the scent and the sound,
the heavenly speech and the holy song,
were heard, the great glory of God,
revelry after revelry. That island trembled,   1325
the earthly plain burst forth. Then the servant, bereft of
courage, became afraid; the unhappy man left quickly
and boarded a boat,
drove the wave-steed; the ship journeyed out,
quick under sorrows. The sun shone hotly,   1330
bright above the dwellings; the ship hurried,
light, striving forward on the journey; the ladened
sea-horse hastened to harbor so that the sea-ship
after the tossing on the sea tread upon the sandy shore,
ground to land. He felt grief   1335
hot in his heart, a sad mind,
a weary mood, he who knew that his master,
his dear friend, remained behind,
bereft of life. The sound of lamentation bitterly
reminded him of that. The tears welled up in waves,   1340
hot drops on his cheeks, and he suffered great sorrow
in his chest. To the maiden, he had to
take the tidings, the hateful yet true message.
Sad in soul, he came then to where the woman was,
the joyous virgin of glory. He did not conceal what had   1345
      happened,
the onward journey of the one fated to die. Needing his

wine-þearfende,   ond þæt word acwæð:
"Ellen biþ selast   þam þe oftost sceal
dreogan dryhten-bealu,   deope behycgan
1350   þroht þeoden-gedal,   þonne seo þrag cymeð,
wefen wyrd-stafum   Þæt wat se þe sceal
aswæman sarig-ferð,   wat his sinc-giefan
holdne biheledne.   He sceal hean þonan
geomor hweorfan.   Þam bið gomenes wana
1355   ðe þa earfeða   oftost dreogeð
on sargum sefan.   Huru, ic swiðe ne þearf
hinsiþ behlehhan.   Is hlaford min,
beorna bealdor,   ond broþor þin,
se selesta   bi sæm tweonum
1360   þara þe we on Engle   æfre gefrunen
acennedne   þurh cildes had
gumena cynnes,   to Godes dome,
werigra wraþu,   woruld-dreamum of,
wine-mæga wyn,   in wuldres þrym,
1365   gewiten, winiga hleo,   wica neosan
eardes on up-weg.   Nu se eorðan dæl,
ban-hus abrocen   burgum in innan
wunað wæl-ræste,   ond se wuldres dæl
of lic-fæte   in leoht Godes
1370   sigor-lean sohte,   ond þe secgan het
þæt git a mosten   in þam ecan gefean
mid þa sib-gedryht   somud-eard niman,
weorca wuldor-lean,   willum neotan
blædes ond blissa.   Eac þe abeodan het
1375   sige-dryhten min,   þa he wæs siþes fus,

friend, he sang a dirge and spoke these words:
"Courage is best for the one who most often has to
endure the loss of his lord, ponder deeply
hardship, the death of his master, when the time comes,   1350
woven by the decrees of fate. He knows that who
must grieve sad at heart, knows that his dear treasure-
giver is buried. Wretched, sorrowing he must turn
away from there. Gladness will be lacking
for him who most often endures hardships   1355
in his grieving heart. Truly, I need not greatly exult
at his death. My lord,
master of men, and your brother,
the best between the seas of those whom we,
of the human race in England, ever heard   1360
born in the form of a child,
the supporter of the weary,
dearest joy of kinsmen, the protector of friends
at the judgment of God has gone from worldly joys
into the majesty of glory to seek an abode   1365
in the land on high. Now the earthly portion,
the broken body, waits inside the building
in its death rest, and the glorious part
has sought the reward of victory in the light
of God away from the body, and he asked me to say   1370
that you two will always have a common home
in that eternal joy with the peaceful host, a glorious
reward for your works, will always enjoy according to
your desires prosperity and bliss. My victorious
lord when he was ready for the journey   1375

73

þæt þu his lic-homan,   leofast mægða,
eorðan biðeahte.   Nu þu ædre const
sið-fæt minne.   Ic sceal sarig-ferð,
hean-mod hweorfan,   hyge drusendne...."
. . . .

also asked that I direct you, dearest maiden,
to cover his body with earth. Now you fully
know my mission. Sad at heart,
downcast, I have to turn away with drooping spirit . . ."

. . . .

JULIANA
The Martyrdom of St. Juliana of Nicomedia

Hwæt, we ðæt hyrdon   hæleð eahtian,
deman dæd-hwate,   þætte in dagum gelamp
Maximianes,   se geond middan-geard,
arleas cyning,   eahtnysse ahof,
5   cwealde cristne men,   circan fylde,
geat on græs-wong   God-hergendra,
hæþen hild-fruma,   haligra blod,
ryht-fremmendra.   Wæs his rice brad,
wid ond weorðlic   ofer wer-þeode,
10   lytesna ofer ealne   yrmenne grund.
Foron æfter burgum,   swa he biboden hæfde,
þegnas þryðfulle.   Oft hi þræce rærdon,
dædum gedwolene,   þa þe Dryhtnes æ
feodon þurh firen-cræft.   Feondscype rærdon,
15   hofon hæþen-gield,   halge cwelmdon,
breotun boc-cræftge,   bærndon gecorene,
gæston Godes cempan   gare ond lige.
Sum wæs æht-welig   æþeles cynnes
rice gerefa.   Rond-burgum weold,
20   eard weardade   oftast symle
in þære ceastre   Commedia,
heold hord-gestreon.   Oft he hæþen-gield
ofer word Godes,   weoh gesohte
neode geneahhe.   Wæs him noma cenned
25   Heliseus,   hæfde ealdordom

Indeed, we have heard men, bold in deeds,
declare and proclaim what happened in the days of
Maximian, the cruel king, the heathen battle-leader,
he who throughout middle-earth raised up persecution,
killed Christian men, felled churches,   5
spilled on the the grassy plain the blood of the
worshippers of God, of the holy, of the
righteous. His kingdom was broad,
wide and splendid over the nations,
almost over all the spacious ground.   10
His powerful attendants traveled through the towns,
as he had commanded. They often engaged in violence,
perverse deeds, those who through wickedness
hated the law of the Lord. They exalted enmity,
raised up heathen idols, slew the holy,   15
destroyed the learned, burned the chosen,
persecuted the soldiers of God with spear and flame.
One of noble lineage was rich,
a powerful reeve. He ruled the fortified towns,
most often inhabited his dwelling place   20
in the city of Nicomedia,
held the treasure hoard. Often in disobedience to God
he very eagerly resorted to heathen idols,
images. His name was
Eleusius; he had great and famous   25

micelne ond mærne.   Ða his mod ongon
fæmnan lufian   (hine fyrwet bræc),
Iulianan.   Hio in gæste bær
halge treowe,   hogde georne
30   þæt hire mægðhad   mana gehwylces
fore Cristes lufan   clæne geheolde.
Ða wæs sio fæmne   mid hyre fæder willan
welegum biweddad;   wyrd ne ful cuþe,
freondrædenne   hu heo from hogde,
35   geong on gæste.   Hire wæs Godes egsa
mara in gemyndum   þonne eall þæt maþþum-gesteald
þe in þæs æþelinges   æhtum wunade.
Þa wæs se weliga   þære wif-gifta,
gold-spedig guma,   georn on mode,
40   þæt him mon fromlicast   fæmnan gegyrede,
bryd to bolde.   Heo þæs beornes lufan
fæste wiðhogde,   þeah þe feoh-gestreon
under hord-locan,   hyrsta unrim
æhte ofer eorþan.   Heo þæt eal forseah
45   ond þæt word acwæð   on wera mengu:
"Ic þe mæg gesecgan   þæt þu þec sylfne ne þearft
swiþor swencan.   Gif þu soðne God
lufast ond gelyfest,   ond his lof rærest,
ongietest gæsta hleo,   ic beo gearo sona
50   unwaclice   willan þines.
Swylce ic þe secge,   gif þu to sæmran gode
þurh deofol-gield   dæde biþencest,
hætsð hæþen-weoh,   ne meaht þu habban mec,
ne geþreatian   þe to gesingan.

dominion. Then his mind began
to love the maiden Juliana (desire tormented him).
In her soul she carried
the holy faith and earnestly determined
that she would keep her virginity pure   30
from each of sins for her love for Christ.
Then the maiden, at her father's wish, was betrothed
to the rich man; he could not really see how things
would turn out, how averse she was, young in spirit,
to affection. To her, fear of God was   35
greater in her thoughts than all the treasure
in the noble's possession.
Then the rich one, the wealthy man,
was eager in his heart for marriage,
eager that the maiden should most speedily be   40
prepared for him, the bride for his home. She resolutely,
firmly rejected the man's love although he owned
treasure in coffer, countless jewels,
on earth. She despised all that
and spoke these words to the multitude of men: 45
"I can tell you that you need not
distress yourself further. If you love and
believe in the true God and exalt his praise,
recognize the Protector of souls, I will be
resolutely prepared for your will.   50
I also say to you, if through idolatry you
devote your acts to a worse god,
make promises to heathen idols, you cannot have me
nor force me to be a wife to you.

55 Næfre þu þæs swiðlic   sar gegearwast
þurh hæstne nið   heardra wita,
þæt þu mec onwende   worda þissa."
Ða se æþeling wearð   yrre gebolgen,
firen-dædum fah,   gehyrde þære fæmnan word,
60 het ða gefetigan   ferend snelle,
hreoh ond hyge-blind,   haligre fæder,
recene to rune.   Reord up astag,
siþþan hy togædre   garas hlændon,
hilde-þremman.   Hæðne wæron begen
65 synnum seoce,   sweor ond aþum.
Ða reordode   rices hyrde
wið þære fæmnan fæder   frecne mode,
darað-hæbbende: "Me þin dohtor hafað
geywed orwyrðu.   Heo me on an sagað
70 þæt heo mæg-lufan   minre ne gyme,
freondrædenne.   Me þa fraceðu sind
on mod-sefan   mæste weorce,
þæt heo mec swa torne   tæle gerahte
fore þissum folce,   het me fremdne god,
75 ofer þa oþre   þe we ær cuþon,
welum weorþian,   wordum lofian,
on hyge hergan,   oþþe hi nabban."
Geswearc þa swið-ferð   swor æfter worde,
þære fæmnan fæder,   ferð-locan onspeon:
80 "Ic þæt geswerge   þurh soð godu,
swa ic are æt him   æfre finde,
oþþe, þeoden,   æt þe þine hyldu
win-burgum in,   gif þas word sind soþ,
monna leofast,   þe þu me sagast,

Never, through violent hatred, will you   55
prepare such severe pain of hard torments
that you might turn me from these words."
Then the noble, guilty of crimes, fierce and spiritually
blind, became swollen with rage on hearing
the woman's words, then commanded a swift messenger   60
to fetch the father of the holy one quickly
to consultation. Speech rose up
after the warriors leaned their spears
together. They were both heathens,
sick with sins, father-in-law and son-in-law.   65
Then the guardian of the kingdom spoke
to the father of the woman with fierce mind,
holding a spear: "Your daughter has
shown dishonor to me. She tells me outright
that she does not care for my love,   70
my affection. To me those insults
are most painful in my heart
that she so grievously should attack me with
blasphemy before this people; she commands me to
worship with riches, praise with words, exalt in mind 75
a strange god over the others
that we knew before or not have her."
The violent-minded one darkened, swore in words,
the maiden's father opened his heart-coffer:
"I swear through the true gods,   80
so ever I may find favor with them,
or, prince, your grace from you
in the wine-cities, if those words are true,
dearest of men, which you speak to me,

85 þæt ic hy ne sparige,   ac on spild giefe,
þeoden mæra,   þe to gewealde.
Dem þu hi to deaþe,   gif þe gedafen þince,
swa to life læt,   swa þe leofre sy."
Eode þa fromlice   fæmnan to spræce,
90 an-ræd ond yfel-þweorg,   yrre gebolgen,
þær he glæd-mode   geonge wiste
wic weardian.   He þa worde cwæð:
"Ðu eart dohtor min   seo dyreste
ond seo sweteste   in sefan minum,
95 ange for eorþan,   minra eagna leoht,
Iuliana.   Þu on geaþe hafast
þurh þin orlegu   unbiþyrfe
ofer witena dom   wisan gefongen.
Wiðsæcest þu to swiþe   sylfre rædes
100 þinum bryd-guman,   se is betra þonne þu,
æþelra for eorþan,   æht-spedigra
feoh-gestreona.   He is to freonde god.
Forþon is þæs wyrþe   þæt þu þæs weres frige,
ece ead-lufan,   an ne forlæte."
105 Him þa seo eadge   ageaf ondsware,
Iuliana   (hio to Gode hæfde
freondrædenne   fæste gestaþelad):
"Næfre ic þæs þeodnes   þafian wille
mægrædenne,   nemne he mægna God
110 geornor bigonge   þonne he gen dyde,
lufige mid lacum   þone þe leoht gescop,
heofon ond eorðan   ond holma bigong,
eodera ymbhwyrft.   Ne mæg he elles mec
bringan to bolde.   He þa bryd-lufan

that I will not spare her, but will give her to   85
destruction, great prince, will give her into
your power. Condemn her to death, if it seems suitable
to you, or allow her life, whichever may be more pleasing
to you." Single-minded and very angry, swollen with rage,
he then went boldly to speak with the virgin,   90
where he knew the glad-hearted, young one
had her place of residence. He then spoke in words:
"You, my daughter, are the dearest
and the sweetest in my heart,
the only one on earth, the light of my eyes,   95
Juliana. You in foolishness have
through your pride against
the judgment of the wise taken a vain course.
You refuse too quickly by your own counsel
your bridegroom, who is better than you,   100
nobler on earth, wealthier in
treasures. He is good as a friend.
Therefore it is worth it for you that you not lose
the man's love, his eternal blessed affection."
The blessed one, Juliana, gave answer   105
(she had firmly committed
her conjugal love to God):
"I will never consent to alliance with the prince
unless he should more eagerly worship the God
of hosts than he has yet done, should   110
love with sacrifices the one who created light,
heaven and earth and the expanse of the seas,
the circuit of the regions. Otherwise he cannot
bring me to his residence. With his possessions, he

115   sceal to oþerre   æht-gestealdum
      idese secan;   nafað he ænige her."
      Hyre þa þurh yrre   ageaf ondsware
      fæder feondlice,   nales frætwe onheht:
      "Ic þæt gefremme,   gif min feorh leofað
120   gif þu unrædes   ær ne geswicest,
      ond þu fremdu godu   forð bigongest
      ond þa forlætest   þe us leofran sind,
      þe þissum folce   to freme stondað,
      þæt þu ungeara   ealdre scyldig
125   þurh deora gripe   deaþe sweltest,
      gif þu geþafian nelt   þing-rædenne,
      modges gemanan.   Micel is þæt ongin
      ond þrea-niedlic   þinre gelican,
      þæt þu forhycge   hlaford urne."
130   Him þa seo eadge   ageaf ondsware,
      gleaw ond Gode leof,   Iuliana:
      "Ic þe to soðe   secgan wille,
      bi me lifgendre   nelle ic lyge fremman.
      Næfre ic me ondræde   domas þine,
135   ne me weorce sind   wite-brogan,
      hilde-woman,   þe þu hæstlice
      man-fremmende   to me beotast,
      ne þu næfre gedest   þurh gedwolan þinne
      þæt þu mec acyrre   from Cristes lofe."
140   Ða wæs ellen-wod,   yrre ond reþe,
      frecne ond ferð-grim,   fæder wið dehter.
      Het hi þa swingan,   susle þreagan,
      witum wægan,   ond þæt word acwæð:

must seek bridal love from another   115
woman; he will not have any here."
To her then in anger her father
gave answer in a hostile manner, not at all a promise of
treasure: "I will bring it about if I live,
if you do not beforehand cease from the ill-advised   120
course, and if you henceforth worship alien gods
and reject those who are dearer to us,
who stand as a help to this people,
that you soon, being forfeit of life,
through the grip of beasts will die the death,   125
if you will not submit to the marriage proposal,
union with the brave man. Great is that undertaking
and calamitous for such as you,
that you should disdain our lord."
To him the blessed one, Juliana,   130
wise and beloved of God, gave answer:
"I will tell you the truth;
while I live, I will not tell a lie.
I will never fear your decrees,
nor are the fearful torments painful to me,   135
the terrors, which you, doing evil,
violently threaten against me,
nor will you ever bring it about through your delusion
that you should turn me from the praise of Christ."
Then furious, angry and fierce, horrible and stern   140
in mind, father was set against daughter.
He ordered her scourged, afflicted with torment,
tortured with punishments, and said these words:

"Onwend þec in gewitte,   ond þa word oncyr
145 þe þu unsnyttrum   ær gespræce,
þa þu goda ussa   gield forhogdest."
Him seo unforhte   ageaf ondsware
þurh gæst-gehygd,   Iuliana:
"Næfre þu gelærest   þæt ic leasingum,
150 dumbum ond deafum   deofol-gieldum,
gæsta geniðlum   gaful onhate,
þam wyrrestum   wites þegnum,
ac ic weorðige   wuldres Ealdor
middan-geardes   ond mægen-þrymmes,
155 ond him anum to   eal biþence,
þæt he mund-bora   min geweorþe
helpend ond hælend   wið hell-sceaþum."
Hy þa þurh yrre   Affricanus,
fæder fæmnan ageaf   on feonda geweald
160 Heliseo.   He in æringe
gelædan het   æfter leohtes cyme
to his dom-setle.   Duguð wafade
on þære fæmnan wlite,   folc eal geador.
Hy þa se æðeling   ærest grette,
165 hire bryd-guma,   bliþum wordum:
"Min se swetesta   sunnan scima,
Iuliana!   Hwæt, þu glæm hafast,
ginfæste giefe,   geoguðhades blæd!
Gif þu godum ussum   gen gecwemest,
170 ond þe to swa mildum   mund-byrd secest,
hyldo to halgum,   beoð þe ahylded fram
wraþe geworhtra   wita unrim,

"Change your thoughts and amend those words
that you unwisely spoke earlier   145
when you disdained the worship of our gods."
To him Juliana, unafraid, gave answer
through her thought:
"You will never teach me to pay tribute to deceiving,
dumb and deaf devil-idols,   150
to the enemies of souls,
to the worst servants of torment,
but I will honor the Lord of glory,
of middle-earth and of majesty,
and in him alone will entrust all,   155
that he will be my protector,
helper and savior against hellish foes."
Then in his rage Affricanus,
the virgin's father, gave her into the power
of enemies, to Eleusius. At daybreak, after   160
the coming of light, he commanded her led
to his judgment seat. The multitude, all the people
together, looked in amazement on the maiden's beauty.
The nobleman, her bridegroom, then first
greeted her in pleasant words: 165
"My sweetest splendor of the sun,
Juliana! How much you have of radiance,
abundant grace, glory of youth!
If you will yet propitiate our gods
and seek their protection so mild,   170
favor from the holy ones, from you will be averted
a countless number of cruelly wrought torments,

grimra gyrna,   þe þe gegearwad sind,
gif þu onsecgan nelt   soþum gieldum."
175 Him seo æþele mæg   ageaf ondsware:
"Næfre þu geþreatast   þinum beotum,
ne wita þæs fela   wraðra gegearwast,
þæt ic þeodscype   þinne lufie,
buton þu forlæte   þa leasinga,
180 weoh-weorðinga,   ond wuldres God
ongyte gleawlice,   gæsta scyppend,
meotud mon-cynnes,   in þæs meahtum sind
a butan ende   ealle gesceafta."
Ða for þam folce   frecne mode
185 beot-wordum spræc,   bealg hine swiþe
folc-agende,   ond þa fæmnan het
þurh nið-wræce   nacode þennan,
ond mid sweopum swingan   synna lease.
Ahlog þa se here-rinc,   hosp-wordum spræc:
190 "Þis is ealdordom   uncres gewynnes
on fruman gefongen.   Gen ic feores þe
unnan wille,   þeah þu ær fela
unwærlicra   worda gespræce,
onsoce to swiðe   þæt þu soð godu
195 lufian wolde.   Þe þa lean sceolan
wiþer-hycgendre,   wite-brogan,
æfter weorþan,   butan þu ær wiþ hi
geþingige,   ond him þonc-wyrþe
æfter leahtor-cwidum   lac onsecge,
200 sibbe gesette.   Læt þa sace restan,
lað leod-gewin.   Gif þu leng ofer þis
þurh þin dol-willen   gedwolan fylgest,
þonne ic nyde sceal   niþa gebæded

of horrible evils, which are prepared for you
if you will not sacrifice to the true dieties."
To him the noble young woman gave answer: 175
"You will never bring it about by your threats
nor prepare so many cruel torments
that I should love your instruction,
unless you let go of those deceiving things,
those sacrifices, and wisely acknowledge   180
the God of glory, the creator of souls,
the measurer of mankind, in whose power are
always without end all created things."
Then before the people with a fierce spirit
he spoke threats, the leader swelled greatly   185
and ordered the maiden free from sins
through severe punishment stretched out naked
and scourged with whips.
Then the warrior laughed, spoke words of contempt:
"Supremacy in our struggle   190
is seized from the start. Yet I still want to grant
you life, although you earlier spoke
many incautious words,
denied too strongly that you would love
the true gods. For your having antagonistic thoughts   195
there must be a reward of fearful torments
unless you should settle with them
and make sacrifice to them with words of thanks
after your blasphemies,
establish peace. Let the dispute,   200
the hateful strife, rest. If you
in your foolishness follow delusion longer about this,
then by necessity, constrained by enmity, I have to

on þære grimmestan   god-scyld wrecan,
205   torne teon-cwide,   þe þu tælnissum
wiþ þa selestan   sacan ongunne,
ond þa mildestan   þara þe men witen,
þe þes leodscype   mid him longe bieode."
Him þæt æþele mod   unforht oncwæð:
210   "Ne ondræde ic me   domas þine,
awyrged wom-sceaða,   ne þinra wita bealo.
Hæbbe ic me to hyhte   heofon-rices weard,
mildne mund-boran,   mægna waldend,
se mec gescyldeð   wið þinum scinlace
215   of gromra gripe,   þe þu to godum tiohhast.
Ða sind geasne   goda gehwylces,
idle, orfeorme,   unbiþyrfe,
ne þær freme meteð   fira ænig
soðe sibbe,   þeah þe sece to him
220   freond-rædenne.   He ne findeð þær
duguþe mid deoflum.   Ic to Dryhtne min
mod staþelige,   se ofer mægna gehwylc
waldeð wide-ferh,   wuldres agend,
sigora gehwylces.   Þæt is soð cyning."
225   Ða þam folc-togan   fracuðlic þuhte
þæt he ne meahte   mod oncyrran,
fæmnan fore-þonc.   He bi feaxe het
ahon ond ahebban   on heanne beam,
þær seo sun-sciene   slege þrowade,
230   sace sin-grimme,   siex tida dæges,
ond he ædre het   eft asettan,
lað-geniðla,   ond gelædan bibead
to carcerne.   Hyre wæs Cristes lof

avenge on you the most horrible impiety,
the grievous, hurtful speech, with which you   205
blasphemously set about to strive against the best and
the mildest whom men know, whom this people have
long worshipped among themselves."
To him that noble, fearless soul replied:
"I do not fear your decrees,   210
cursed fiend, nor your evil torments.
I have as my hope the guardian of the heavenly
kingdom, the gentle protector, ruler of hosts,
who shields me against your superstition,
from the grip of enemies whom you hold as gods.   215
They are barren of every good,
idle, useless, vain,
nor does any man obtain benefit there,
true peace, although he might seek friendship
for himself. He does not find help there   220
with devils. I will fix my mind upon the Lord,
the ruler of glory, who
always has dominion over each of hosts,
each of victories. That is the true King."
It seemed shameful to the folk-leader   225
that he could not change the mind or
intention of the maiden. He commanded her hung
and hauled up on a high gallows by her hair
where the one radiant as the sun endured a beating,
exceedingly fierce strife, for six hours of the day,   230
and he, hateful oppressor, ordered her to be
taken down again and commanded that she be led
to prison. The praise of Christ,

in ferð-locan   fæste biwunden,
235   milde mod-sefan,   mægen unbrice.
Ða wæs mid clustre   carcernes duru
behliden, homra geweorc.   Halig þær inne
wærfæst wunade.   Symle heo wuldor-cyning
herede æt heortan,   heofon-rices God,
240   in þam nyd-clafan,   nergend fira,
heolstre bihelmad.   Hyre wæs Halig Gæst
singal gesið.   Ða cwom semninga
in þæt hlin-ræced   hæleða gewinna,
yfeles ondwis.   Hæfde engles hiw,
245   gleaw gyrn-stafa   gæst-geniðla,
helle hæftling,   to þære halgan spræc:
"Hwæt dreogest þu,   seo dyreste
ond seo weorþeste   wuldor-cyninge,
Dryhtne ussum?   Ðe þes dema hafað
250   þa wyrrestan   witu gegearwad,
sar endeleas,   gif þu onsecgan nelt,
gleaw-hycgende,   ond his godum cweman.
Wes þu on ofeste,   swa he þec ut heonan
lædan hate,   þæt þu lac hraþe
255   onsecge sigor-tifre,   ær þec swylt nime,
deað fore duguðe.   Þy þu þæs deman scealt,
ead-hreðig mæg,   yrre gedygan."
Frægn þa fromlice,   seo þe forht ne wæs,
Criste gecweme,   hwonan his cyme wære.
260   Hyre se wræc-mæcga   wið þingade:
"Ic eom engel Godes   ufan siþende,

an inviolate power, was firmly enclosed
in her heart, in her gentle mind.   235
Then with a bar, the work of hammers,
the prison door was locked. The holy, faithful one
remained therein. Wrapped in darkness in that narrow
cell, she always praised in her heart the king
of glory, the God of the heavenly kingdom,   240
the savior of souls. The Holy Spirit was
her constant companion. Then suddenly into that hall
of confinement came the adversary of human beings,
skillful in evil. Having the shape of an angel,
the enemy of souls, wise in afflictions,   245
the captive of hell, spoke to the saint:
"Why do you, dearest
and most worthy to the king of glory,
to our Lord, suffer? For you this judge has
prepared the worst punishments,   250
endless torment, if you will not sacrifice,
wise-thinking, and please his gods.
Since he ordered you led out of here,
so you could quickly make an offering, a sacrifice
for deliverance, hurry before destruction seizes you,   255
death before the multitude. By this you will escape,
blessed virgin, the judge's wrath."
Then she boldly asked, she who was not afraid,
pleasing to Christ, where he came from.
The wretch addressed her: 260
"I am an angel of God come from above,

95

þegn geþungen, ond to þe sended,
halig of heahþu. Þe sind heardlicu,
wundrum wel-grim, witu geteohhad
265 to gring-wræce. Het þe God beodan,
bearn waldendes, þæt þe burge þa."
Ða wæs seo fæmne for þam fær-spelle
egsan geaclad, þe hyre se aglæca,
wuldres wiþer-breca, wordum sægde.
270 Ongan þa fæstlice ferð staþelian,
geong grondorleas, to Gode cleopian:
"Nu ic þec, beorna hleo, biddan wille,
ece ælmihtig, þurh þæt æþele gesceap
þe þu, Fæder engla, æt fruman settest,
275 þæt þu me ne læte of lofe hweorfan
þinre ead-gife, swa me þes ar bodað
frecne fær-spel, þe me fore stondeð.
Swa ic þe, bilwitne, biddan wille
þæt þu me gecyðe, cyninga wuldor,
280 þrymmes hyrde, hwæt þes þegn sy,
lyft-lacende, þe mec læreð from þe
on stearcne weg." Hyre stefn oncwæð
wlitig of wolcnum, word hleoþrade:
"Forfoh þone frætgan ond fæste geheald,
285 oþþæt he his siðfæt secge mid ryhte,
ealne from orde, hwæt his æþelu syn."
Ða wæs þære fæmnan ferð geblissad,
dom-eadigre. Heo þæt deofol genom . . .

". . . ealra cyninga cyning to cwale syllan.
290 Ða gen ic gecræfte þæt se cempa ongon

a noble servant, and sent to you,
holy from the heights. Severe,
wondrously cruel torments are decreed for you
as deadly punishments. God ordered that I command   265
you, child of the ruler, that you watch out for those."
Then the virgin was gripped by fear because of
the sudden frightful message that the evil creature,
the adversary of glory, said to her.
Young and innocent, she then began firmly   270
to fix her heart, to call out to God:
"Now protector of men, eternal and almighty,
I will beg you through that noble creation
that you, Father of angels, established at the beginning
that you not let me turn from praise   275
of your grace, since this messenger standing before
me announces a dangerous, frightening message.
So, gentle one, I will beg
you to make known to me, glory of kings,
shepherd of glory, who this servant is,   280
borne on the air, who on your behalf teaches me
to venture onto a rough path." To her a voice,
beautiful from the clouds, replied, spoke in words:
"Seize the wicked one and hold it fast,
until it tells truthfully of his journey,   285
all from the beginning, what his origins are."
Then the heart of the virgin was gladdened,
blessed with glory. She grabbed that devil . . .

". . . give the king of all kings to a violent death.
Then still I contrived that the warrior began   290

97

waldend wundian   —weorud to segon—
þæt þær blod ond wæter   bu tu ætgædre
eorþan sohtun.   Ða gen ic Herode
in hyge bisweop   þæt he Iohannes bibead
295   heafde biheawan,   ða se halga wer
þære wif-lufan   wordum styrde,
unryhtre æ.   Eac ic gelærde
Simon searo-þoncum   þæt he sacan ongon
wiþ þa gecorenan   Cristes þegnas,
300   ond þa halgan weras   hospe gerahte
þurh deopne gedwolan,   sægde hy drys wæron.
Neþde ic nearo-bregdum   þær ic Neron bisweac,
þæt he acwellan het   Cristes þegnas,
Petrus ond Paulus.   Pilatus ær
305   on rode aheng   rodera waldend,
meotud meahtigne   minum larum.
Swylce ic Egias   eac gelærde
þæt he unsnytrum   Andreas het
ahon haligne   on heanne beam,
310   þæt he of galgan his   gæst onsende
in wuldres wlite.   Þus ic wraþra fela
mid minum broþrum   bealwa gefremede,
sweartra synna,   þe ic asecgan ne mæg,
rume areccan,   ne gerim witan,
315   heardra hete-þonca."   Him seo halge oncwæð
þurh Gæstes giefe,   Iuliana:
"Þu scealt furþor gen,   feond mon-cynnes,
siþfæt secgan,   hwa þec sende to me."
Hyre se aglæca   ageaf ondsware,
320   forht afongen,   friþes orwena:
"Hwæt, mec min fæder   on þas fore to þe,

98

wounding the ruler—the crowd looked on—
so that both blood and water
sought the earth together. Then I incited Herod
in his mind to order John's
head cut off, when the holy man   295
rebuked in words his love for a woman,
his unlawful marriage. I also taught
Simon cunningly so that he began to contend
with the chosen servants of Christ
and attacked the holy men with insolence   300
through deep delusion, said they were magicians.
I ventured by means of evil tricks when I seduced Nero
into ordering Christ's attendants killed,
Peter and Paul. Pilate had earlier
hanged on the cross the ruler of the firmament,   305
the mighty measurer, through my teachings.
Likewise I also taught Aegias
to foolishly order the holy Andrew
hanged on a high tree
so that from the gallows he sent his spirit   310
into the beauty of glory. Thus many of cruel evils
with my brothers I performed,
black sins, which I cannot express,
relate in full, nor know the number of
hard, hateful thoughts." To him the holy one, Juliana,   315
replied through the grace of the Spirit:
"You must further yet, enemy of mankind,
relate your errand, who sent you to me."
To her the evil creature gave answer,
gripped by fear, despairing of peace: 320
"Yes, my father, the king of the inhabitants of hell,

hell-warena cyning,   hider onsende
of þam engan ham,   se is yfla gehwæs
in þam grorn-hofe   geornfulra þonne ic.
325 Þonne he usic sendeð   þæt we soðfæstra
þurh misgedwield   mod oncyrren,
ahwyrfen from halor,   we beoð hyge-geomre,
forhte on ferðþe.   Ne biþ us frea milde,
egesful ealdor,   gif we yfles noht
330 gedon habbaþ;   ne durran we siþþan
for his onsyne   ower geferan.
Þonne he onsendeð   geond sidne grund
þegnas of þystrum,   hateð þræce ræran,
gif we gemette sin   on mold-wege,
335 oþþe feor oþþe neah   fundne weorþen,
þæt hi usic binden   ond in bæl-wylme
suslum swingen.   Gif soðfæstra
þurh myrrelsan   mod ne oðcyrreð,
haligra hyge,   we þa heardestan
340 ond þa wyrrestan   witu geþoliað
þurh sar-slege.   Nu þu sylfa meaht
on sefan þinum   soð gecnawan,
þæt ic þisse noþe wæs   nyde gebæded,
þrag-mælum geþread,   þæt ic þe sohte."
345 Þa gen seo halge ongon   hæleþa gewinnan,
wrohtes wyrhtan,   wordum frignan,
fyrn-synna fruman: "Þu me furþor scealt
secgan, sawla feond,   hu þu soðfæstum
þurh synna slide   swiþast sceþþe,
350 facne bifongen."   Hyre se feond oncwæð,
wræcca wærleas,   wordum mælde:

he who is more eager than I in each of evils
in that house of sorrows, sent me here
on this journey to you from that narrow home.
When he sends us to change   325
the hearts of the righteous through evil deceit,
turn them away from salvation, we are sad in mind,
afraid at heart. Nor will he be a gentle lord to us,
the terrible prince, if we have not done anything
evil; we do not dare afterward   330
come into his sight anywhere.
Then he sends servants of darkness
throughout the spacious land, orders them to use
violence, if we should be met on earth,
or should be found far or near,   335
so that they bind us and in surging fire
afflicts us with torments. If the mind of the righteous,
the thought of the holy ones is not changed
through stumbing blocks, we suffer the hardest
and the worst punishments   340
through a painful blow. Now you can
know the truth in your heart yourself,
that I was constrained by necessity to this boldness
in seeking you out, tortured by unhappy times."
Then again in words the holy one began to ask   345
the foe of men, the evildoer,
the originator of ancient sins: "You must tell me
further, enemy of souls, encompassed by evil, how you
most seriously injure the righteous
through falling into sin." To her the enemy,   350
the faithless exile replied, spoke in words:

"Ic þe, ead-mæg,   yfla gehwylces
or gecyðe   oð ende forð
þara þe ic gefremede,   nalæs feam siðum,
355   synna wundum,   þæt þu þy sweotolicor
sylf gecnawe   þæt þis is soð, nales leas.
Ic þæt wende   ond witod tealde
þriste geþoncge,   þæt ic þe meahte
butan earfeþum   anes cræfte
360   ahwyrfan from halor,   þæt þu heofon-cyninge
wiðsoce, sigora Frean,   ond to sæmran gebuge,
onsægde synna fruman.   Þus ic soðfæstum
þurh mislic bleo   mod oncyrre.
Þær ic hine finde   ferð staþelian
365   to Godes willan,   ic beo gearo sona
þæt ic him monigfealde   modes gælsan
ongean bere   grimra geþonca,
dyrnra gedwilda,   þurh gedwolena rim.
Ic him geswete   synna lustas,
370   mæne mod-lufan,   þæt he minum hraþe,
leahtrum gelenge,   larum hyreð.
Ic hine þæs swiþe   synnum onæle
þæt he byrnende   from gebede swiceð,
stepeð stronglice,   staþolfæst ne mæg
375   fore leahtra lufan   lenge gewunian
in gebed-stowe.   Swa ic brogan to
laðne gelæde   þam þe ic lifes ofonn,
leohtes geleafan,   ond he larum wile
þurh modes myne   minum hyran,
380   synne fremman,   he siþþan sceal
godra gum-cysta   geasne hweorfan.

"Blessed virgin, I will make known to you
from beginning to end
each evil that I performed by the wounds of sin,
and not just a few times, so that you will more clearly   355
know that this is true, not at all a lie.
I expected and boldly considered it a certainty
that I could by my own skill
turn you from salvation without difficulty
so that you would renounce the heavenly king   360
the Lord of victories, and bow to a worse one,
sacrifice to the originator of sins. Thus I, through
my various forms, turn the minds of the righteous.
Where I find him fixing his heart
in the will of God, I am immediately ready   365
to bear the manifold lusts of the mind
against him, horrible thoughts,
secret errors, through countless delusions.
For him I make sweet the pleasures of sins,
wicked affection, so that he, attached to vices,   370
will quickly obey my teachings.
I so greatly inflame him with sins
that, burning, he ceases prayer,
boldly steps away, may not for long
remain firm in the place of prayer   375
because of his love of vices. Thus I bring a loathsome
thing as a terror to the one whose life I begrudge,
the light of faith, and if he wants
in the desire of his heart to obey my teachings,
to commit sins, he must then   380
turn away, deprived of excellent virtues.

Gif ic ænigne   ellen-rofne
gemete modigne   metodes cempan
wið flan-þræce,   nele feor þonan
385   bugan from beaduwe,   ac he bord ongean
hefeð hyge-snottor,   haligne scyld,
gæstlic guð-reaf,   nele Gode swican,
ac he beald in gebede   bid-steal gifeð
fæste on feðan,   ic sceal feor þonan
390   hean-mod hweorfan,   hroþra bidæled,
in gleda gripe,   gehðu mænan,
þæt ic ne meahte   mægnes cræfte
guðe wiðgongan,   ac ic geomor sceal
secan oþerne   ellenleasran,
395   under cumbol-hagan,   cempan sænran,
þe ic onbryrdan mæge   beorman mine,
agælan æt guþe.   Þeah he godes hwæt
onginne gæstlice,   ic beo gearo sona,
þæt ic in-gehygd   eal geondwlite,
400   hu gefæstnad sy   ferð innanweard,
wiðer-steall geworht.   Ic þæs wealles geat
ontyne þurh teonan;   bið se torr þyrel,
in-gong geopenad,   þonne ic ærest him
þurh earg-fare   in onsende
405   in breost-sefan   bitre geþoncas
þurh mislice   modes willan,
þæt him sylfum   selle þynceð
leahtras to fremman   ofer lof Godes,
lices lustas.   Ic beo lareow georn
410   þæt he mon-þeawum   minum lifge

If I should meet any courageous
warrior of the measurer,
bold against a storm of arrows, not willing far from there
to flee from battle, but wise in mind he   385
raises a board, a holy shield against me,
spiritual battle gear, not willing to fail God,
but brave in prayer he makes a stand
steadfast in the troop, I must
depart far from there, downcast, deprived of joys,   390
in the grip of burning coals, lament my miseries,
that I could not prevail in battle
by force of might, but sad, I must
seek another, less courageous one
in the phalanx, a worse warrior   395
whom I can incite with my leaven of evil,
hinder in battle. Although he might try something
good spiritually, I am immediately prepared
to scrutinize all his inner thoughts,
how fortified his heart may be inside,   400
how the resistance is constituted. I open the gate
of that wall through malice; the tower is pierced,
the entrance opened; then I first
through the flurry of arrows send into
his heart bitter thoughts   405
through various desires of the mind,
so that to himself it seems better
to practice vices, lusts of the body,
than the praise of God. I am eagerly a teacher
so that he will live by my sinful customs   410

acyrred cuðlice   from Cristes æ,
mod gemyrred   me to gewealde
in synna seað.   Ic þære sawle ma
geornor gyme   ymb þæs gæstes forwyrd
415   þonne þæs lic-homan,   se þe on legre sceal
weorðan in worulde   wyrme to hroþor,
bifolen in foldan."   Ða gien seo fæmne spræc:
"Saga, earm-sceapen,   unclæne gæst,
hu þu þec geþyde,   þystra stihtend,
420   on clænra gemong?   Þu wið Criste geo
wærleas wunne   ond gewin tuge,
hogdes wiþ halgum.   Þe wearð helle seað
niþer gedolfen,   þær þu nyd-bysig
fore ofer-hygdum   eard gesohtes.
425   Wende ic þæt þu þy wærra   weorþan sceolde
wið soðfæstum   swylces gemotes
ond þy unbealdra,   þe þe oft wiðstod
þurh wuldor-cyning   willan þines."
Hyre þa se werga   wið þingade,
430   earm aglæca: "Þu me ærest saga,
hu þu gedyrstig   þurh deop gehygd
wurde þus wig-þrist   ofer eall wifa cyn,
þæt þu mec þus fæste   fetrum gebunde,
æghwæs orwigne.   Þu in ecne God,
435   þrym-sittendne,   þinne getreowdes,
meotud mon-cynnes,   swa ic in minne fæder,
hell-warena cyning,   hyht staþelie.
Þonne ic beom onsended   wið soðfæstum,
þæt ic in man-weorcum   mod oncyrre,
440   hyge from halor,   me hwilum biþ
forwyrned þurh wiþer-steall   willan mines,

clearly turned from the law of Christ,
his mind confused into my power
in the pit of sins. I care more for the soul,
more earnestly about the destruction of the spirit,
than of the body, which must in its grave   415
in the world become a joy to the worm,
buried in the ground." Then the virgin spoke again:
"Tell me, miserable, impure spirit,
disposer of darknesses, how you associated yourself
with the company of the pure? Faithless, for a long time   420
you strove against Christ and created conflict,
busied yourself against the holy. For you the pit of
hell was dug below, where, distressed
because of pride, you sought a dwelling place.
I expected that you would be more on guard   425
and less bold in such a meeting
with the righteous, who often withstood
your will through the king of glory."
Then the accursed one, the wretched creature,
addressed her: "You tell me first   430
how you, bold through deep
reflection, became so daring in battle
above all womankind that you could firmly
bind me, completely defenseless, with fetters in this way.
You fixed your trust in eternal God, sitting in glory,   435
the measurer of humankind, just as I fixed my hope
in my father, king of hell-dwellers.
When I am sent against the righteous
to bend her mind to evil deeds,
her thought from salvation, sometimes it will   440
be to me denied through the holy one's opposing

hyhtes æt halgum,　swa me her gelamp
sorg on siþe.　Ic þæt sylf gecneow
to late micles,　sceal nu lange ofer þis,
445　scyld-wyrcende,　scame þrowian.
　　Forþon ic þec halsige　þurh þæs hyhstan meaht,
rodor-cyninges giefe,　se þe on rode treo
geþrowade,　þrymmes Ealdor,
þæt þu miltsige　me þearfendum,
450　þæt unsælig　eall ne forweorþe,
þeah ic þec gedyrstig　ond þus dol-willen
siþe gesohte,　þær ic swiþe me
þyslicre ær　þrage ne wende."
　　Ða seo wlite-scyne　wuldres condel
455　to þam wærlogan　wordum mælde:
"Þu scealt ondettan　yfel-dæda ma,
hean helle gæst,　ær þu heonan mote,
hwæt þu to teonan　þurhtogen hæbbe
micelra man-weorca　manna tudre
460　deorcum gedwildum."　Hyre þæt deofol oncwæð:
"Nu ic þæt gehyre　þurh þinne hleoþor-cwide,
þæt ic nyde sceal　niþa gebæded
mod meldian,　swa þu me beodest,
þrea-ned þolian.　Is þeos þrag ful strong,
465　þreat ormæte.　Ic sceal þinga gehwylc
þolian ond þafian　on þinne dom,
wom-dæda onwreon,　þe ic wide-ferg
sweartra gesyrede.　Oft ic syne ofteah,
ablende bealo-þoncum　beorna unrim
470　monna cynnes,　mist-helme forbrægd
þurh attres ord　eagna leoman

my will, my hope; and so sorrow befell
me here. I understand that
much too late and must now, evildoing,
long suffer shame over this.   445
Therefore I entreat you through the might of the
most high, by the grace of the king of the firmament,
he who suffered on the cross, the Lord of glory,
that you have mercy on me in my need,
so that, miserable, I should not utterly perish,   450
although rash and foolish in this way
I sought you here in my journey, where I did not
much expect such a time for me before."
Then the radiantly beautiful candle of glory
spoke in words to the traitor: 455
"You must confess more evil deeds,
wretched hell-spirit, before you may leave here,
what you have perpetrated of great evil works
to the injury of the children of humanity
through dark delusions." To her the devil said: 460
"Now I hear through your voice
that by necessity, impelled by afflictions, I must
reveal my mind, as you order me,
suffer punishment. This occasion is very powerful,
the oppression boundless. I must suffer   465
each of things and submit to your judgment,
uncover black, shameful deeds that I ever
devised. Often I removed the sight,
blinded with evil thoughts a countless number
of people, of humankind, covered with a helmet of mist   470
the light of the eyes through a poisonous shaft

sweartum scurum,   ond ic sumra fet
forbræc bealo-searwum,   sume in bryne sende,
in liges locan,   þæt him lasta wearð
475   siþast gesyne.   Eac ic sume gedyde
þæt him ban-locan   blode spiowedan,
þæt hi færinga   feorh aleton
þurh ædra wylm.   Sume on yð-fare
wurdon on wege   wætrum bisencte,
480   on mere-flode,   minum cræftum
under reone stream.   Sume ic rode bifealh,
þæt hi heoro-dreorge   on hean galgan
lif aletan.   Sume ic larum geteah,
to geflite fremede,   þæt hy færinga
485   ealde æfþoncan   edniwedan,
beore druncne.   Ic him byrlade
wroht of wege,   þæt hi in win-sele
þurh sweord-gripe   sawle forletan
of flæsc-homan   fæge scyndan,
490   sarum gesohte.   Sume, þa ic funde
butan Godes tacne,   gymelease,
ungebletsade,   þa ic bealdlice
þurh mislic cwealm   minum hondum
searo-þoncum slog.   Ic asecgan ne mæg,
495   þeah ic gesitte   sumer-longne dæg,
eal þa earfeþu   þe ic ær ond siþ
gefremede to facne,   siþþan furþum wæs
rodor aræred   ond ryne tungla,
folde gefæstnad   ond þa forman men,
500   Adam ond Aeue—   þam ic ealdor oðþrong,
ond hy gelærde   þæt hi lufan Dryhtnes,

with dark showers, and I crushed the feet of some
with wicked snares, sent some into the fire,
into the captivity of flame, so that was the last seen
of their tracks. I also afflicted some   475
so that ther bodies spurted blood,
and they suddenly gave up their lives
through the gushing of the veins. Some
by my powers on a sea journey were submerged in waters,
on the way, on the ocean,   480
under the dismal stream. Some I gave over to the cross,
so that they, covered with blood,
gave up their life on the high gallows. Some I have incited
by my teaching, brought to strife, so that they
suddenly renewed old grudges,   485
having drunk beer. I served them
sin from a cup so that they
through the grip of swords in the wine-hall let
their souls hasten from their bodies fated to die,
assailed with wounds. Some whom I found   490
without God's mark, careless,
unblessed, those I boldly
and cunningly slew through various deaths
by my own hands. I cannot tell
even if I should sit the summer-long day,   495
all the hardships that I always
caused through evil, since the firmament
and the course of the stars were raised up,
the earth was established as well as the first humans,
Adam and Eve—I took life from them by force,   500
and they learned that they had relinquished the love

III

ece ead-giefe   anforleton,
beorhtne bold-welan,   þæt him bæm gewearð
yrmþu to ealdre,   ond hyra eaferum swa,
505   mircast man-weorca.   Hwæt sceal ic ma riman
yfel endeleas?   Ic eall gebær,
wraþe wrohtas   geond wer-þeode,
þa þe gewurdun   widan feore
from fruman worulde   fira cynne,
510   eorlum on eorþan.   Ne wæs ænig þara
þæt me þus þriste,   swa þu nuþa,
halig mid hondum,   hrinan dorste,
næs ænig þæs modig   mon ofer eorþan
þurh halge meaht,   heah-fædra nan
515   ne witgena.   Þeah þe him weoruda God
onwrige, wuldres cyning,   wisdomes Gæst,
giefe unmæte,   hwæþre ic gong to þam
agan moste.   Næs ænig þara
þæt mec þus bealdlice   bennum bilegde,
520   þream forþrycte,   ær þu nuþa
þa miclan meaht   mine oferswiðdest,
fæste forfenge,   þe me fæder sealde,
feond mon-cynnes,   þa he mec feran het,
þeoden of þystrum,   þæt ic þe sceolde
525   synne swetan.   Þær mec sorg bicwom,
hefig hond-gewinn.   Ic bihlyhhan ne þearf
æfter sar-wræce   siðfæt þisne
magum in gemonge,   þonne ic mine sceal
agiefan gnorn-cearig   gaful-rædenne
530   in þam reongan ham."   Ða se gerefa het,

of the Lord, the eternal gift of prosperity,
the bright splendid dwelling; that, the blackest
of wicked deeds, became a misery for both of them
forever, and for their offspring as well. Why should I   505
recount more of endless evil? I started it all,
all the cruel sins among nations,
those that have always befallen
the race of men, the people of earth,
from the beginning of the world. None of them   510
was as bold, as you, holy one, are now, that
they would dare touch me with their hands,
nor was anyone across the face of the earth as courageous
through holy might, none of the patriarchs
nor of the prophets. Although the God of hosts,   515
the king of glory, the Spirit of wisdom
revealed the immeasurable gift to them, I was still
allowed access to them. None of them
so boldly covered me with bonds,
oppressed me with abuse before you now   520
when you vanquished my great might,
firmly seized what my father,
the enemy of humankind, gave me when he ordered me,
a prince from the darkness, to go sweeten
sins for you. Sorrow met me there,   525
heavy hand-combat. After grievous
persecution I do not need to exult about this journey
among my kinsmen when I, troubled,
have to yield up my tribute
in that sad home." Then the reeve,   530

gealg-mod guma,   Iulianan
of þam engan hofe   ut gelædan
on hyge halge   hæþnum to spræce
to his dom-setle.   Heo þæt deofol teah,
535   breostum inbryrded,   bendum fæstne,
halig hæþenne.   Ongan þa hreow-cearig
siðfæt seofian,   sar cwanian,
wyrd wanian;   wordum mælde:
"Ic þec halsige,   hlæfdige min,
540   Iuliana,   fore Godes sibbum,
þæt þu furþur me   fraceþu ne wyrce,
edwit for eorlum,   þonne þu ær dydest,
þa þu oferswiþdest   þone snotrestan
under hlin-scuan   hel-warena cyning
545   in feonda byrig;   þæt is fæder user,
morþres man-frea.   Hwæt, þu mec þreades
þurh sar-slege.   Ic to soþe wat
þæt ic ær ne sið   ænig ne mette
in woruld-rice   wif þe gelic,
550   þristran geþohtes   ne þweorh-timbran
mægþa cynnes.   Is on me sweotul
þæt þu unscamge   æghwæs wurde
on ferþe frod."   Ða hine seo fæmne forlet
æfter þræc-hwile   þystra neosan
555   in sweartne grund,   sawla gewinnan,
on wita forwyrd.   Wiste he þi gearwor,
manes melda,   magum to secgan,
susles þegnum,   hu him on siðe gelomp.

          . . . .

                    . . . "georne ær
560   heredon on heahþu   ond his halig weorc,

the gallows-minded man, commanded Juliana
led out from that narrow hall
holy in mind to speak to the heathen
at his judgment seat. Ardent in heart, she dragged
that devil along fastened in bonds, the holy one,   535
the heathen. Then, troubled, he began
to lament the journey, bewail his sorrow,
bemoan what had happened; he spoke in words:
"I entreat you, my lady
Juliana, by the grace of God,   540
that you inflict no further insults on me,
disgrace before men, than you previously did,
when you conquered the wisest king of
hell-dwellers in the prison,
in the city of enemies; that is our father,   545
the evil prince of murder. Indeed, you afflicted me
through painful blows. I know for certain
that I have never met
in the worldly kingdom any woman like you,
more daring of thought nor more resolutely made   550
among young women. It is clear from my example
that you, completely unashamed, have become
wise in heart." Then the virgin let him,
the adversary of souls, after his time of misery
go seek darkness in the black abyss, in the destruction   555
of torments. He, the reporter of wickedness,
knew the more readily to tell his
kinsmen, the servants of torment, what happened to him
on the journey . . .

                  ". . . [whom] earnestly before
they had praised on high and his holy work,   560

115

sægdon soðlice   þæt he sigora gehwæs
ofer ealle gesceaft   ana weolde,
ecra ead-giefa." Ða cwom engel Godes
frætwum blican   ond þæt fyr tosceaf,
565   gefreode ond gefreoðade   facnes clæne,
leahtra lease,   ond þone lig towearp,
heoro-giferne,   þær seo halie stod,
mægþa bealdor,   on þam midle gesund.
Þæt þam weligan wæs   weorc to þolianne,
570   þær he hit for worulde   wendan meahte;
sohte synnum fah,   hu he sarlicast
þurh þa wyrrestan   witu meahte
feorh-cwale findan.   Næs se feond to læt,
se hine gelærde   þæt he læmen fæt
575   biwyrcan het   wundor-cræfte,
wiges womum,   ond wudu-beamum,
holte bihlænan.   Ða se hearda bibead
þæt mon þæt lam-fæt   leades gefylde,
ond þa onbærnan het   bæl-fira mæst,
580   ad onælan;   se wæs æghwonan
ymbboren mid brondum.   Bæð hate weol.
Het þa ofestlice   yrre gebolgen
leahtra lease   in þæs leades wylm
scufan butan scyldum.   Þa toscaden wearð
585   lig tolysed.   Lead wide sprong,
hat, heoro-gifre.   Hæleð wurdon acle
arasad for þy ræse.   Þær on rime forborn
þurh þæs fires fnæst   fif ond hundseofontig
hæðnes herges.   Ða gen sio halge stod
590   ungewemde wlite.   Næs hyre wloh ne hrægl,

said truly that he alone had dominion
over each of victories across all creation,
over the eternal gifts of grace." Then came the angel of
God shining with adornments and thrust aside that fire,
freed and defended the one pure of crime,   565
devoid of faults, and cast away the flame,
greedy for slaughter, where the holy one,
the lord of maidens, stood unharmed within.
For the wealthy man that was a distress to endure,
as to whether for all the world he could change it;   570
stained with sins, he looked for how he most sorely
through the worst punishments might
devise her violent death. The enemy was not too slow;
he instructed him to have
a clay vessel made by miraculous power, have it   575
set around with the terrible sounds of battle, and with
forest trees, with timber. Then the hard man ordered
the clay vessel filled with lead,
and then commanded the greatest bonfire lit,
a pyre kindled; it was everywhere   580
surrounded with flames. The bath boiled with heat.
Swollen with rage, he suddenly ordered
the one devoid of faults, without guilt, to be pushed
into the surging lead. Then the fire was separated,
set free. Lead burst out widely,   585
hot, fiercely ravenous. The men were seized
by fear before the onslaught.
Consumed there by the blast of fire were seventy-five
of the heathen host. Still, the holy one stood
in uninjured beauty. Neither hem nor garment,   590

ne feax ne fel   fyre gemæled,
ne lic ne leoþu.   Heo in lige stod
æghwæs onsund,   sægde ealles þonc
dryhtna Dryhtne.   Þa se dema wearð

595   hreoh ond hyge-grim,   ongon his hrægl teran,
swylce he grennade   ond gristbitade,
wedde on gewitte   swa wilde deor,
grymetade gealg-mod   ond his godu tælde,
þæs þe hy ne meahtun   mægne wiþstondan

600   wifes willan.   Wæs seo wuldres mæg
an-ræd ond unforht,   eafoða gemyndig,
Dryhtnes willan.   Þa se dema het
aswebban sorg-cearig   þurh sweord-bite
on hyge halge,   heafde bineotan

605   Criste gecorene.   Hine se cwealm ne þeah,
siþþan he þone fintan   furþor cuþe.
Ða wearð þære halgan   hyht geniwad
ond þæs mægdnes mod   miclum geblissad,
siþþan heo gehyrde   hæleð eahtian

610   inwit-rune,   þæt hyre ende-stæf
of gewin-dagum   weorþan sceolde,
lif alysed.   Het þa leahtra ful
clæne ond gecorene   to cwale lædan,
synna lease.   Ða cwom semninga

615   hean helle gæst,   hearm-leoð agol,
earm ond unlæd,   þone heo ær gebond
awyrgedne   ond mid witum swong,
cleopade þa for corþre,   cear-gealdra full:
"Gyldað nu mid gyrne,   þæt heo goda ussa

neither hair nor skin, neither body nor limbs
was marred by fire. She stood in the flame,
completely whole, giving thanks for everything
to the Lord of lords. Then the judge became
stormy and savage in mind, began to tear his clothes;   595
he also bared his teeth and gnashed them,
raged in his mind like a wild beast,
gallows-minded reviled and reproached his gods
because they could not withstand through might
the will of the woman. The virgin of glory was   600
resolute and unafraid, mindful of powers,
of the will of the Lord. Then the wretched judge
ordered her, holy in mind, put to death through
the sword's bite, Christ's chosen one deprived of
her head. That slaying did not profit him   605
when he later experienced its consequences.
Then hope was renewed for the holy one
and the mind of the virgin greatly blessed
when she heard the man deliberate
in evil counsel that the end   610
of her days of trouble would occur,
her life set free. Then the one full of vices
commanded the pure and chosen one, the one
without sin, led to a violent death. Suddenly
a wretched spirit from hell came, sang a lamentation,   615
miserable and accursed, the corrupted one whom she had
previously bound and afflicted with torments, called
out before the troop, full of sorrowful incantations:
"Repay her now with trouble because she

620 meaht forhogde,   ond mec swiþast
geminsade,   þæt ic to meldan wearð.
Lætað hy laþra   leana hleotan
Þurh wæpnes spor,   wrecað ealdne nið,
synne gesohte.   Ic þa sorge gemon,
625 hu ic bendum fæst   bisga unrim
on anre niht   earfeða dreag,
yfel ormætu."   Þa seo eadge biseah
ongean gramum,   Iuliana,
gehyrde heo hearm galan   helle deofol.
630 Feond mon-cynnes   ongon þa on fleam sceacan,
wita neosan,   ond þæt word acwæð:
"Wa me forworhtum.   Nu is wen micel
þæt heo mec eft wille   earmne gehynan
yflum yrmþum,   swa heo mec ær dyde."
635 Ða wæs gelæded   lond-mearce neah
ond to þære stowe   þær hi stearc-ferþe
þurh cumbol-hete   cwellan þohtun.
Ongon heo þa læran   ond to lofe trymman
folc of firenum   ond him frofre gehet,
640 weg to wuldre,   ond þæt word acwęð:
"Gemunað wigena wyn   ond wuldres þrym,
haligra hyht,   heofon-engla God.
He is þæs wyrðe,   þæt hine wer-þeode
ond eal engla cynn   up on roderum
645 hergen, heah-mægen,   þær is help gelong
ece to ealdre,   þam þe agan sceal.
Forþon ic, leof weorud,   læran wille,
æ-fremmende,   þæt ge eower hus
gefæstnige,   þy læs hit fer-blædum

despised the power of our gods and greatly diminished   620
me so that I became an informer.
Let her have the hated rewards through
wounds, avenge the old strife,
enveloped by sin. I remember that sorrow,
how held fast in bonds, I suffered in one night   625
a countless number of afflictions, of miseries,
boundless evil." When the blessed Juliana looked
toward the fierce one, she heard the
devil from hell sing misery.
The enemy of humankind then took flight   630
to seek his punishments and spoke these words:
"Woe to me, all undone. The probability
is great now that she will torment wretched me again
with evil miseries just as she did before."
Then she was led close to the boundary land   635
to the place where they intended to kill
the strong-hearted one with hateful violence.
Then she began to teach and encourage the people
from sins to praise and promised them comfort,
a path to glory, speaking these words: 640
"Remember the joy of warriors and splendor of glory,
the hope of the holy, the God of the heavenly angels.
He is worthy that the nations of men and
all the race of angels up in the firmament
should praise him, the high power, where help is   645
present for ever and ever for the one who will have it.
Therefore, dear people, in my piety I want to teach
you to make fast your house lest with
sudden blasts the wind should
destroy it. A strong wall must the more firmly   650

650 windas toweorpan.   Weal sceal þy trumra
strong wiþstondan   storma scurum,
leahtra gehygdum.   Ge mid lufan sibbe,
leohte geleafan,   to þam lifgendan
stane stið-hydge   staþol fæstniað,
655 soðe treowe   ond sibbe mid eow
healdað æt heortan,   halge rune
þurh modes myne.   Þonne eow miltse giefeð
Fæder ælmihtig,   þær ge freme agun
æt mægna Gode,   mæste þearfe
660 æfter sorg-stafum.   Forþon ge sylfe neton
ut-gong heonan,   ende lifes.
Wærlic me þinceð   þæt ge wæccende
wið hettendra   hilde-woman
wearde healden,   þy læs eow wiþer-feohtend
665 weges forwyrnen   to wuldres byrig.
Biddað Bearn Godes   þæt me brego engla,
meotud mon-cynnes,   milde geweorþe,
sigora sellend.   Sibb sy mid eowic,
symle soþ lufu."   Ða hyre sawl wearð
670 alæded of lice   to þam langan gefean
þurh sweord-slege.   Þa se syn-scaþa
to scipe sceoh-mod   sceaþena þreate,
Heliseus,   eh-stream sohte,
leolc ofer lagu-flod   longe hwile
675 on swon-rade.   Swylt ealle fornom
secga hloþe   ond hine sylfne mid,
ærþon hy to lande   geliden hæfdon,
þurh þearlic þrea.   Þær þrittig wæs
ond feowere eac   feores onsohte

withstand the showers of storms,
the thoughts of vices. With the peace of love,
with the light of faith, resolutely establish
a foundation on the living stone, hold
a true belief and peace among you   655
in your hearts, holy secrets
with purpose of mind. Then the Father
almighty will give you grace where you have most need
of comfort after anxieties from the
God of strengths. For you do not know   660
the exit from here, the end of life.
It seems prudent to me that you being watchful
against the battle clashes of the enemies
should keep up your guard lest the adversaries
block your way to the city of glory.   665
Beseech the Son of God that the ruler of angels,
the creator of humankind, the giver of victories,
be merciful to me. Peace be with you,
true love forever." Then her soul was
escorted from her body to the lasting joy   670
through the thrust of a sword. Then fearful of heart the
miscreant Eleusius with a band of warriors
went to sea by ship,
tossed on the waves for a long time
on the swan-road. Death took them all,   675
the troop of men and him, too,
as a severe punishment
before they reached land. There
thirty of the warrior kind and four besides
were deprived of life through the billowing of the wave; 680

680 þurh wæges wylm   wigena cynnes,
heane mid hlaford,   hroþra bidæled,
hyhta lease   helle sohton.

Ne þorftan þa þegnas   in þam þystran ham,
seo geneat-scolu   in þam neolan scræfe,
685 to þam frum-gare   feoh-gestealda
witedra wenan,   þæt hy in win-sele
ofer beor-setle   beagas þegon,
æpplede gold.   Ungelice wæs
læded lof-songum   lic haligre
690 micle mægne   to mold-græfe,
þæt hy hit gebrohton   burgum in innan,
sid-folc micel.   Þær siððan wæs
geara gongum   Godes lof hafen
þrymme micle   oþ þisne dæg
695 mid þeodscipe.   Is me þearf micel
þæt seo halge me   helpe gefremme,
þonne me gedælað   deorast ealra,
sibbe toslitað   sinhiwan tu,
micle mod-lufan.   Min sceal of lice
700 sawul on siðfæt,   nat ic sylfa hwider,
eardes uncyðþu;   of sceal ic þissum,
secan oþerne   ær-gewyrhtum,
gongan iu-dædum.   Geomor hweorfeð
ᚳ ᚪ ond ᛏ.   Cyning biþ reþe,
705 sigora syllend,   þonne synnum fah
ᛗ ᚹ ond ᚾ   acle bidað
hwæt him æfter dædum   deman wille
lifes to leane.   ᛚ ᚠ beofað,

wretched with their lord, bereft of joys,
without hope, they went to hell.
The servants in that dark home,
the band of attendants in that deep pit,
had no need to expect from that leader   685
their allotted riches, or that they
along the beer-bench would receive rings,
embossed gold in the wine-hall. With songs of praise,
the body of the holy one was led to the grave
in a different manner by a great host when they,   690
a great mass of people, brought it
inside the town. There afterward
in the course of time the praise of God was raised up
with great splendor until this day
among the people. For me there is a great need   695
that the saint should give me help,
when the most beloved of all to me
the united pair, part their bond,
their great affection. My soul must depart from my
body on a journey in ignorance, to what land   700
I know not where; I must from this land
seek another with my past works,
journey with my former deeds. Mournful,
ᚳ, ᚪ, and ᛏ will depart. The king, the giver of victories,
will be harsh when, stained with sins,   705
ᛗ, ᚹ, and ᚾ terrified await
what he wishes to decree for them as a reward
for their lives according to their deeds. ᚢ, ᛚ
wretched will shake, tremble. I remember all

seomað sorg-cearig.   Sar eal gemon,
710 synna wunde,   þe ic siþ oþþe ær
geworhte in worulde.   Þæt ic wopig sceal
tearum mænan.   Wæs an tid to læt
þæt ic yfel-dæda   ær gescomede,
þenden gæst ond lic   geador siþedan
715 on sund on earde.   Þonne arna biþearf,
þæt me seo halge   wið þone hyhstan cyning
geþingige.   Mec þæs þearf monaþ,
micel modes sorg.   Bidde ic monna gehwone
gumena cynnes,   þe þis gied wræce,
720 þæt he mec neodful   bi noman minum
gemyne modig   ond Meotud bidde
þæt me heofona helm   helpe gefremme,
meahta waldend,   on þam miclan dæge,
Fæder, frofre Gæst,   in þa frecnan tid,
725 dæda demend,   ond se deora Sunu,
þonne seo Þrynis   þrym-sittende
in annesse   ælda cynne
þurh þa sciran gesceaft   scrifeð bi gewyrhtum
meorde monna gehwam.   Forgif us, mægna God,
730 þæt we þine onsyne,   æþelinga wyn,
milde gemeten   on þa mæran tid.
Amen.

the suffering, the wounds of sin, that late or early   710
I caused in the world. Mournful, I must lament that
with tears. I was too late at the time
in feeling shame for evil deeds
while my spirit and body journeyed together
in health on earth. Therefore I will have need of favors   715
for the saint to intercede for me with the highest
king. My need, my great sorrow of mind,
reminds me of this. I pray everyone
of the human race, earnest and noble-minded,
who recites this poem will remember   720
me by name and pray the Lord
that he, the protector of the heavens,
the wielder of powers, will help me in that great day,
the Father, the Spirit of consolation, in that dangerous
hour, the judge of deeds, and the dear Son,   725
when the Trinity dwelling in glory in
unity will decree for the human race
throughout the bright creation a reward according to
works for each person. Grant us, God of
hosts, joy of princes, that we might find your face   730
gentle in that great hour.
Amen.

THE FATES OF
THE APOSTLES

Hwæt. Ic þysne sang   sið-geomor fand
on seocum sefan,   samnode wide
hu þa æðelingas   ellen cyðdon,
torhte ond tir-eadige.   Twelfe wæron,
5   dædum domfæste,   Dryhtne gecorene,
leofe on life.   Lof wide sprang,
miht ond mærðo,   ofer middan-geard,
þeodnes þegna,   þrym unlytel.
Halgan heape   hlyt wisode
10   þær hie Dryhtnes æ   deman sceoldon,
reccan fore rincum.   Sume on Rome-byrig,
frame, fyrd-hwate,   feorh ofgefon
þurg Nerones   nearwe searwe,
Petrus ond Paulus.   Is se apostolhad
15   wide geweorðod   ofer wer-þeoda.
Swylce Andreas   in Achagia
for Egias   aldre geneðde.
Ne þreodode he fore þrymme   ðeod-cyninges,
æniges on eorðan,   ac him ece geceas
20   langsumre lif,   leoht unhwilen,
syþþan hilde-heard,   heriges byrhtme,
æfter guð-plegan   gealgan þehte.
Hwæt, we eac gehyrdon   be Iohanne
æ-glæawe menn   æðelo reccan.
25   Se manna wæs,   mine gefrege,

Listen. Journey-weary, I devised this song
in my sick heart, gathered widely
how the champions, bright and glorious,
made their courage known. There were twelve,
renowned in deeds, chosen by the Lord,   5
dear to him in life. Their glory spread widely,
the might and fame of the prince's disciples,
no small majesty, across the earth.
Their lot guided the holy troop to
where they must proclaim the law of the Lord,   10
expound it before warriors. Notable men in Rome,
bold, warlike, gave up their lives
through Nero's cunning treachery,
Peter and Paul. Apostleship is
widely honored among the people.   15
Likewise Andrew in Achaia
risked his life before Ægias.
He did not turn before the might of the
king, of anyone on earth, but chose for himself
eternal, more enduring life, timeless light,   20
when to the shouting of the army, battle-hard,
he stretched across the cross after war-play.
Listen, we have also heard men versed in scripture
expound about John, about his lineage.
Of humans in the shape of a man   25

þurh cneorisse   Criste leofast
on weres hade,   syððan wuldres cyning,
engla ord-fruma,   eorðan sohte
þurh fæmnan hrif,   Fæder mann-cynnes.
30 He in Effessia   ealle þrage
leode lærde;   þanon lifes weg
siðe gesohte,   swegle dreamas,
beorhtne bold-welan.   Næs his broðor læt,
siðes sæne,   ac ðurh sweordes bite
35 mid Iudeum   Iacob sceolde
fore Herode   ealdre gedælan,
feorh wið flæsce.   Philipus wæs
mid Asseum;   þanon ece lif
þurh rode cwealm   ricene gesohte,
40 syððan on galgan   in Gearapolim
ahangen wæs   hilde-corðre.
Huru, wide wearð   wurd undyrne
þæt to Indeum   aldre gelædde
beadu-cræftig beorn,   Bartholameus;
45 þone heht Astrias   in Albano,
hæðen ond hyge-blind,   heafde beneotan,
forþan he ða hæðen-gild   hyran ne wolde,
wig weorðian.   Him wæs wuldres dream,
lif-wela leofra   þonne þas leasan godu.
50 Swylce Thomas eac   þriste geneðde
on Indea   oðre dælas,
þær manegum wearð   mod onlihted,
hige onhyrded,   þurh his halig word.
Syððan collen-ferð   cyninges broðor

I have heard he was dearest to Christ because of
his family, after the king of glory,
the creator of angels, visited the earth
by means of a virgin's womb, the Father of humankind.
All the time in Ephesus, he   30
taught the people; from there, he sought in time
the path of life, radiant joys,
the bright happy home. His brother was not slow,
reluctant for the journey, but through the bite
 of the sword among the Jews, James had to   35
part from life before Herod,
to separate spirit from flesh. Philip was
among the Asians; from there he sought
eternal life at once through death on the cross,
after on the gallows in Hierapolis   40
he was hanged by a band of armed men.
Truly, the event became widely known
that Bartholomew, valiant in battle,
went to live in India;
Astrages, heathen and blind in heart, commanded   45
him in Albanapolis to be deprived of his head,
because he did not want to follow the heathen rite,
sacrifice to idols. For him the joy of glory,
of the happy life was dearer than those false gods.
Likewise Thomas also ventured boldly   50
in the other parts of India,
where for many the heart was illuminated,
the mind encouraged through his holy word.
Then the bold-hearted one raised up the king's brother

55 awehte for weorodum, wundor-cræfte,
þurh Dryhtnes miht, þæt he of deaðe aras,
geong ond guð-hwæt, ond him wæs Gad nama;
ond ða þæm folce feorg gesealde,
sin æt sæcce. Sweord-ræs fornam
60 þurh hæðene hand, þær se halga gecrang,
wund for weorudum, þonon wuldres leoht
sawle gesohte sigores to leane.
Hwæt, we þæt gehyrdon þurg halige bec
þæt mid Sigel-warum soð yppe wearð,
65 dryhtlic dom Godes. Dæges or onwoc,
leohtes geleafan, land wæs gefælsod
þurh Matheus mære lare.
Þone het Irtacus ðurh yrne hyge,
wæl-reow cyning, wæpnum aswebban.
70 Hyrde we þæt Iacob in Ierusalem
fore sacerdum swilt þrowode;
ðurg stenges sweng stið-mod gecrang,
eadig for æfestum. Hafað nu ece lif
mid wuldor-cining, wiges to leane.
75 Næron ða twegen tohtan sæne,
lind-gelaces, land Persea
sohton sið-frome, Simon ond Thaddeus,
beornas beado-rofe. Him wearð bam samod
an ende-dæg. Æðele sceoldon
80 ðurh wæpen-hete weorc þrowigan,
sige-lean secan, ond þone soðan gefean,
dream æfter deaðe, þa gedæled wearð

before the hosts by marvelous skill, through 55
the power of the Lord, so that he rose from death,
young and bold in battle, and his name was Gad;
and Thomas yielded up his life then to the people
in strife. A sword attack by a heathen hand
took him, where the saint fell, 60
wounded before the multitudes; from there with his soul
he sought the light of glory as a reward for victory.
Listen, we have heard through holy books
that among the Ethiopians the truth was revealed,
the noble glory of God. Dawn awakened, 65
belief in the light, the land was cleansed
through the renowned teaching of Matthew.
Irtacus, the savage king, through
an angry mind, ordered him killed with weapons.
We have heard that James in Jerusalem 70
before the priests suffered death;
through the blow of a club the resolute one fell,
blessed on account of the acts of malice. He has eternal
life now with the glorious king as a reward for war.
These two were not slow to battle, 75
to the play of shields; the eager ones sought
the land of Persia, Simon and Thaddeus,
the warriors valiant in battle. One day was for them both
together the last. The noble ones had to
suffer pain through armed hostility, 80
to seek the reward of victory and the true happiness,
joy after death, when life was separated

lif wið lice,   ond þas lænan gestreon,
idle æht-welan,   ealle forhogodan.
85   Ðus ða æðelingas   ende gesealdon,
twelfe til-modige.   Tir unbræcne
wegan on gewitte   wuldres þegnas.
Nu ic þonne bidde   beorn se ðe lufige
þysses giddes begang   þæt he geomrum me
90   þone halgan heap   helpe bidde,
friðes ond fultomes.   Huru, ic freonda beþearf
liðra on lade,   þonne ic sceal langne ham,
eard-wic uncuð,   ana gesecean,
lætan me on laste   lic, eorðan dæl,
95   wæl-reaf wunigean   weormum to hroðre.
Her mæg findan   fore-þances gleaw,
se ðe hine lysteð   leoð-giddunga,
hwa þas fitte fegde.   ᚠ þær on ende standeþ;
eorlas þæs on eorðan brucaþ.   Ne moton hie awa
                    ætsomne,
100   woruld-wunigende.   ᚹ sceal gedreosan,
ᚢ on eðle;   æfter tohweorfan
læne lices frætewa,   efne swa ᛚ toglideð
þonne ᚳ ond ᚣ   cræftes neotað
nihtes nearowe;   on him ᚾ ligeð,
105   cyninges þeodom.   Nu ðu cunnon miht
hwa on þam wordum wæs   werum oncyðig.
Sie þæs gemyndig,   mann se ðe lufige
þisses galdres begang,   þæt he geoce me
ond frofre fricle.   Ic sceall feor heonan,
110   an elles forð,   eardes neosan,

from body, and they entirely disdained this transitory
treasure, this idle hoarded wealth.
Thus the nobles gave up their end,   85
twelve good-hearted ones. The servants of glory
bore unbreakable renown in their mind.
Now then I bid whoever takes pleasure
in the content of this poem that he should bid
the holy troop for help for my mournful self,   90
for peace and protection. Indeed, I need friends,
kind ones, on the journey, when I alone have to
seek the long-lasting home, the unknown dwelling,
to leave my body behind, this portion of earth,
the spoil of slaughter to remain as a comfort for worms.   95
Here one wise of forethought,
one who delights in poetic songs, can discover
who composed this song. ᚠ stands at the end;
men enjoy that on earth. But they cannot always
be together, dwelling in the world. ᚢ must pass away,   100
ᚾ in the native land; after that the transitory adornments
of the body will disperse, even as the ᛚ vanishes
when ᛣ and ᚻ exercise strength
with labor in the night; ᛏ lies upon them,
the service of the king. Now you can know   105
who has been made known to people in these words.
May the person who enjoys the content
of this song be mindful of it and ask for help
and relief for me. I must go far from here,
alone on the way forth, seek a dwelling,   110

sið asettan,   nat ic sylfa hwær,
of þisse worulde.   Wic sindon uncuð,
eard ond eðel,   swa bið ælcum menn
nemþe he godcundes   gastes bruce.

115   Ah utu we þe geornor   to Gode cleopigan,
sendan usse bene   on þa beorhtan gesceaft,
þæt we þæs botles   brucan motan,
hames in hehðo;   þær is hihta mæst,
þær cyning engla   clænum gildeð

120   lean unhwilen.   Nu a his lof standeð,
mycel ond mære,   ond his miht seomaþ,
ece ond edgiong,   ofer ealle gesceaft.

FINIT.

take a journey from this world,
I do not know where. The habitations are unknown,
the dwelling and the land, as they are to everyone
unless he or she partakes of a divine spirit.
But let us more eagerly call to God,   115
send our petitions into the bright creation,
so that we might enjoy the dwelling,
the home in the heights; there the greatest of hopes is,
where the king of angels grants to the pure
timeless reward. Now and forever his glory stands,   120
great and famous, and his power will remain,
eternal and ageless, throughout all creation.

FINIT.

ELENE

The Finding of the True Cross

Þa wæs agangen   geara hwyrftum
tu hund ond þreo   geteled rimes,
swylce þrittig eac,   þing-gemearces,
wintra for worulde,   þæs þe wealdend God
5   acenned wearð,   cyninga wuldor,
in middan-geard   þurh mennisc heo,
soðfæstra leoht.   Þa wæs syxte gear
Constantines   caserdomes
þæt he Rom-wara   in rice wearð
10   ahæfen hild-fruma,   to here-teman.
Wæs se leod-hwata   lind-geborga
eorlum arfæst.   Æðelinges weox
rice under roderum.   He wæs riht cyning,
guð-weard gumena.   Hine God trymede
15   mærðum ond mihtum,   þæt he manegum wearð
geond middan-geard   mannum to hroðer,
wer-þeodum to wræce,   syððan wæpen ahof
wið hetendum.   Him wæs hild boden,
wiges woma.   Werod samnodan
20   Huna leode   ond Hreð-gotan,
foron fyrd-hwate   Francan ond Hugas.
Wæron hwate weras,
gearwe to guðe.   Garas lixtan,
wriðene wæl-hlencan.   Wordum ond bordum

Then in the course of years and reckoning
in numbers and periods of time
two hundred and thirty-three
winters had passed in this world since the ruling God,
the light of the faithful, the glory of kings,   5
had been born in middle-earth in human form.
It was the sixth year
of Constantine's reign
since he was raised up prince in the kingdom
of the Romans as a leader.   10
The courageous warrior was
honorable to men. The prince's kingdom grew
under the firmament. He was a true king,
a warlord of men. God confirmed him
in glories and in strengths so he became to many people   15
throughout middle-earth a comfort,
but a misery to nations when he raised a weapon
against enemies. Battle was offered him,
the noise of war. The Hunnish people
and the Hrethgoths assembled their troops,   20
the brave Franks and Hugas went forth.
The men were brave,
ready for war. The spears shone,
the woven coats of mail. With words and shields,

25   hofon here-combol.   Þa wæron heardingas
      sweotole gesamnod   ond eal sib geador.
      For folca gedryht.   Fyrd-leoð agol
      wulf on wealde,   wæl-rune ne mað.
      Urig-feðera   earn sang ahof,
30   laðum on laste.   Lungre scynde
      ofer burgende   beadu-þreata mæst,
      hergum to hilde,   swylce Huna cyning
      ymb-sittendra   awer meahte
      abannan to beadwe   burg-wigendra.
35   For fyrda mæst   —feðan trymedon—
      eored-cestum,   þæt on ælfylce
      deareð-lacende   on Danubie,
      stærced-fyrhðe,   stæðe wicedon
      ymb þæs wæteres wylm   werodes breahtme.
40   Woldon Rom-wara   rice geþringan,
      hergum ahyðan.   Þær wearð Huna cyme
      cuð ceasterwarum.   Þa se casere heht
      ongean gramum   guð-gelæcan
      under earh-fære   ofstum myclum
45   bannan to beadwe,   beran ut þræce
      rincas under roderum.   Wæron Rom-ware,
      secgas sige-rofe,   sona gegearwod
      wæpnum to wigge,   þeah hie werod læsse
      hæfdon to hilde   þonne Huna cining;

they raised the battle standard. Then the warriors 25
and all the kin were clearly gathered together.
The company of folk moved forward. The wolf chanted
the battle song in the forest, did not conceal the slaughter
rune. The dewy-feathered eagle raised a song
in pursuit of the hateful ones. The greatest of troops 30
hastened at once across the city boundary
toward the armies in battle that the king of the Huns,
of the neighbors, of the city-dwellers, could
summon anywhere to the fight.
The greatest of armies advanced in bands of chosen men 35
—drew into formation—so that in the foreign nation
resolute warriors on the Danube
encamped on the bank
around the surging water to the acclaim of the troop.
They wanted to throng into the empire of the Romans, 40
to plunder it with the armies. There the coming of the
       Huns became
known to the city-dwellers. Then the emperor
       commanded
the warriors summoned with great haste to battle against
the fierce ones under the flight of arrows,
commanded the soldiers to proceed into the fray 45
under the firmament. The Romans,
the triumphant men, were immediately prepared
with weapons for war although they had a smaller
army for the conflict than did the king of the Huns;

50 ridon ymb rofne.   Þonne rand dynede,
camp-wudu clynede,   cyning þreate for,
herge to hilde.   Hrefen uppe gol,
wan ond wæl-fel.   Werod wæs on tyhte.
Hleopon horn-boran,   hreopan friccan,
55 mearh moldan træd.   Mægen samnode,
cafe to cease.   Cyning wæs afyrhted,
egsan geaclad,   siððan el-þeodige,
Huna ond Hreða   here sceawedon
ðæt he on Rom-wara   rices ende
60 ymb þæs wæteres stæð   werod samnode,
mægen unrime.   Mod-sorge wæg
Rom-wara cyning,   rices ne wende
for werodleste,   hæfde wigena to lyt,
eaxl-gestealna   wið ofer-mægene,
65 hrora to hilde.   Here wicode,
eorlas ymb æðeling,   eg-streame neah
on neaweste   niht-langne fyrst,
þæs þe hie feonda gefær   fyrmest gesægon.
Þa wearð on slæpe   sylfum ætywed
70 þam casere,   þær he on corðre swæf,
sige-rofum gesegen   swefnes woma.
Þuhte him wlite-scyne   on weres hade
hwit ond hiw-beorht,   hæleða nathwylc
geywed ænlicra   þonne he ær oððe sið
75 gesege under swegle.   He of slæpe onbrægd,
eofur-cumble beþeaht.   Him se ar hraðe,

they rode around the renowned one. Then the shield   50
     resounded,
the battle-wood clattered, the king advanced with the
troop, with the army, to battle. The raven cried aloft,
dark and fierce. The company was on the march.
The trumpeters ran, the heralds called out,
the horse tread the ground. The host gathered   55
swift to the conflict. The king was afraid,
filled with terror after the foreigners, the horde
of Huns and Hrethgoths, saw that he had
assembled a host, a limitless force
by the water's shore at the edge of the Romans'   60
realm. The king of the Romans felt sorrow,
did not expect victory
for lack of troops; he had too few warriors,
shoulder-companions, against the superior strength
of the bold ones in battle. The army,   65
the men around the prince, encamped close to
the river for the night,
once they saw their enemies' expedition.
Then in sleep was revealed to the emperor himself
where he slept among his troop, to the triumphant   70
one was made apparent the revelation of a dream.
It seemed to him that a beautiful creature appeared in
the form of a man, white and bright of hue,
a certain warrior more peerless than he
had ever seen beneath the sky. He started from sleep,   75
covered by his boar banner. Immediately the messenger,

wlitig wuldres boda,   wið þingode
ond be naman nemde,   —niht-helm toglad:
"Constantinus,   heht þe cyning engla,
80   wyrda wealdend,   wære beodan,
duguða Dryhten.   Ne ondræd þu ðe,
ðeah þe elþeodige   egesan hwopan,
heardre hilde.   Þu to heofenum beseoh
on wuldres weard,   þær ðu wraðe findest,
85   sigores tacen."   He wæs sona gearu
þurh þæs halgan hæs   —hreðer-locan onspeon—
up locade   swa him se ar abead,
fæle friðo-webba.   Geseah he frætwum beorht
wliti wuldres treo   ofer wolcna hrof,
90   golde geglenged,   —gimmas lixtan.
Wæs se blaca beam   boc-stafum awriten,
beorhte ond leohte: "Mid þys beacne ðu
on þam frecnan fære   feond oferswiðesð,
geletest lað werod."   Þa þæt leoht gewat,
95   up siðode,   ond se ar somed,
on clænra gemang.   Cyning wæs þy bliðra
ond þe sorgleasra,   secga aldor,
on fyrhð-sefan   þurh þa fægeran gesyhð.

II

Heht þa onlice   æðelinga hleo,
100   beorna beag-gifa,   swa he þæt beacen geseah,
heria hild-fruma,   þæt him on heofonum ær
geiewed wearð,   ofstum myclum,

the beautiful emissary of glory, spoke with him
and called him by name—the helmet of night had
departed: "Constantine, the king of angels,
the ruler of fates, the Lord of hosts, commanded   80
his covenant offered to you. Do not dread,
although foreign nations may threaten you with terror,
with hard battle. Look to the heavens
to the Guardian of glory, where you will find help,
a symbol of victory." He was immediately prepared   85
from the command of the holy one—he opened his
       breast—
and looked up as the messenger, the true peace-weaver,
had bid him. He saw bright with treasures
the beautiful tree of glory above the vault of the clouds,
adorned with gold—the gems glistened.   90
The shining tree was inscribed with letters,
brightly and clearly: "With this sign you
will overcome the enemy in the terrible expedition,
you will withstand the hateful troop." Then that light
and the messenger with it, departed, journeyed upward,   95
into the company of the pure. The king, the leader of the
men, was all the happier and less sorrowful
in his heart because of that fair vision.

                                                     II

Then the protector of princes,
the ring-giver of men, the glorious king, Constantine,   100
ordered a sign made with great haste
in the likeness of Christ's cross,

Constantinus,   Cristes rode,
tir-eadig cyning,   tacen gewyrcan.

105 Heht þa on uhtan   mid ær-dæge
wigend wreccan,   ond wæpen-þræce
hebban heoru-cumbul,   ond þæt halige treo
him beforan ferian   on feonda gemang,
beran beacen Godes.   Byman sungon

110 hlude for hergum.   Hrefn weorces gefeah;
urig-feðra   earn sið beheold,
wæl-hreowra wig.   Wulf sang ahof,
holtes gehleða.   Hild-egesa stod.
Þær wæs borda gebrec   ond beorna geþrec,

115 heard hand-geswing   ond herga gring,
syððan heo earh-fære   ærest metton.
On þæt fæge folc   flana scuras,
garas ofer geolo-rand   on gramra gemang,
hetend heoru-grimme,   hilde-nædran,

120 þurh fingra geweald   forð onsendan.
Stopon stið-hidige,   stundum wræcon,
bræcon bord-hreðan,   bil in dufan,
þrungon þræc-hearde.   Þa wæs þuf hafen,
segn for sweotum,   sige-leoð galen.

125 Gylden grima,   garas lixtan
on here-felda.   Hæðene grungon,
feollon friðelease.   Flugon instæpes
Huna leode,   swa þæt halige treo
aræran heht   Rom-wara cyning,

130 heaðo-fremmende.   Wurdon heardingas
wide towrecene.   Sume wig fornam.

just as the battle-leader of armies saw that symbol
which had been revealed to him before in the heavens.
Then at first light of dawn he ordered   105
the warriors roused
to raise the standard in battle and carry that holy tree,
bear the sign of God before them
among their enemies. The trumpets sang loudly before
the armies. The raven rejoiced in the armies' work;   110
dewy-feathered, the eagle beheld the event,
the war of the cruel ones. The wolf raised a song,
the companion of the wood. Battle-terror grew.
There was the crash of shields and tumult of men,
hard combat and slaughter of armies,   115
after they first met the flight of arrows.
Into that fated folk, the very fierce foe through the
power of fingers sent forth showers of arrows, spears,
battle-serpents over the yellow shields
into the crowd of fierce ones.   120
Stouthearted they advanced, at times pressed forward,
broke the phalanx, thrust in the sword,
the brave ones thronged. Then the standard was raised,
the banner before the troops, a victory song chanted.
Golden helmets and spears shone   125
on the battlefield. The heathens died,
fell without protection. Right away the people
of the fighting Huns fled as the king
of the Romans ordered that holy tree
lifted up. The warriors were   130
widely scattered. Battle took some.

Sume unsofte   aldor generedon
on þam here-siðe.   Sume healf-cwice
flugon on fæsten   ond feore burgon
æfter stan-clifum,   stede weardedon
ymb Danubie.   Sume drenc fornam
on lago-streame   lifes æt ende.
Ða wæs modigra   mægen on luste;
ehton el-þeoda   oð þæt æfen forð
fram dæges orde.   Daroð-æsc flugon,
hilde-nædran.   Heap wæs gescyrded,
laðra lind-wered.   Lythwon becwom
Huna herges   ham eft þanon.
Þa wæs gesyne   þæt sige forgeaf
Constantino   cyning ælmihtig
æt þam dæg-weorce,   dom-weorðunga,
rice under roderum,   þurh his rode treo.
Gewat þa heriga helm   ham eft þanon,
huðe hremig,   —hild wæs gesceaden—
wigge geweorðod.   Com þa wigena hleo
þegna þreate   þryð-bord steran,
beadu-rof cyning   burga neosan.
Heht þa wigena weard   þa wisestan
snude to sionoðe,   þa þe snyttro cræft
þurh fyrn-gewrito   gefrigen hæfdon,
heoldon hige-þancum   hæleða rædas.
Ða þæs fricggan ongan   folces aldor,
sige-rof cyning,   ofer sid weorod,
wære þær ænig   yldra oððe gingra

135

140

145

150

155

Some with difficulty saved their lives
in that campaign. Some half-alive
fled to safety along the stony cliffs and protected
their lives, guarded a place   135
by the Danube. Drowning took some
in the river at the end of life.
Then the host of courageous ones was pleased;
until evening from the break of day,
they pursued the foreign nation. Spears of ash wood,   140
battle adders, flew. The troop was destroyed,
the shield band of the hateful ones. Few of the army
of the Huns came home from there again.
Then it was seen that the king almighty
gave victory to Constantine   145
for that day's work, honor, power
under the skies, through his cross. The protector of armies
departed home again from there,
exulting in plunder— the battle was decided—
made worthy by war. The refuge of warriors then came   150
with his throng of attendants to steer his mighty ship,
the war-renowned king to seek his cities.
The guardian of warriors then commanded the wisest
men quickly to assembly, those who had learned
the craft of wisdom through ancient writings,   155
kept the counsel of heroes in their thoughts.
Then the prince of the people, the victory-renowned
king, began to ask across the broad troop
if there was anyone, old or young,

160 þe him to soðe   secggan meahte,
galdrum cyðan,   hwæt se god wære,
boldes brytta,   "þe þis his beacen wæs
þe me swa leoht oðywde   ond mine leode generede,
tacna torhtost,   ond me tir forgeaf,
165 wig-sped wið wraðum,   þurh þæt wlitige treo."
Hio him ondsware   ænige ne meahton
agifan togenes,   ne ful geare cuðon
sweotole gesecggan   be þam sige-beacne.
Þa þa wisestan   wordum cwædon
170 for þam here-mægene   þæt hit heofon-cyninges
tacen wære,   ond þæs tweo nære.
Þa þæt gefrugnon   þa þurh fulwihte
lærde wæron,   —him wæs leoht sefa,
ferhð gefeonde,   þeah hira fea wæron—
175 ðæt hie for þam casere   cyðan moston
godspelles gife,   hu se gasta helm,
in Þrynesse   þrymme geweorðad,
acenned wearð,   cyninga wuldor,
ond hu on galgan wearð   Godes agen Bearn
180 ahangen for hergum   heardum witum.
Alysde leoda bearn   of locan deofla,
geomre gastas,   ond him gife sealde
þurh þa ilcan gesceaft   þe him geywed wearð
sylfum on gesyhðe,   sigores tacne,
185 wið þeoda þræce;   ond hu ðy þriddan dæge
of byrgenne   beorna wuldor
of deaðe aras,   Dryhten ealra
hæleða cynnes,   ond to heofonum astah.

who might tell him, the ruler of the palace,   160
as a truth, make known in speeches who
the god might be "whose sign this was
that was revealed so bright to me and saved my people,
the brightest of symbols, and gave me glory,
success in war against the hostile ones by means of that   165
beautiful tree." They could not give him any answer
nor fully were able exactly
to speak clearly about that victory sign.
Then the wisest spoke in words
before the multitude that it was the sign   170
of the heavenly king, and of that there was no doubt.
Then those who had been taught through baptism
—their mind was clear,
their heart rejoicing, though they were few—
heard that they had to make known to the emperor   175
the gift of the gospel, how the protector of spirits,
the glory of kings, honored in the majesty
of the Trinity, was born,
and how God's only Son was hanged
on the gallows before the multitudes with cruel torments.   180
He released the sons of the people, the sorrowful souls,
from the imprisonment of devils and gave to them grace
through that same object that had been revealed
before his very eyes, by the sign of victory,
against the attack of nations; and how on the third day   185
from the tomb the glory of men
the Lord of all mankind
rose from the dead and ascended into heaven.

Đus gleawlice   gast-gerynum
190 sægdon sige-rofum,   swa fram Siluestre
lærde wæron.   Æt þam se leod-fruma
fulwihte onfeng   ond þæt forð geheold
on his dagana tid   dryhtne to willan.

III

Đa wæs on sælum   sinces brytta,
195 nið-heard cyning.   Wæs him niwe gefea
befolen in fyrhðe;   wæs him frofra mæst
ond hyhta hihst   heofon-rices weard.
Ongan þa Dryhtnes æ   dæges ond nihtes
þurh Gastes gife   georne cyðan,
200 ond hine soðlice   sylfne getengde
gold-wine gumena   in Godes þeowdom,
æsc-rof, unslaw.   Þa se æðeling fand,
leod-gebyrga,   þurh lar-smiðas,
guð-heard, gar-þrist,   on Godes bocum
205 hwær ahangen wæs   heriges beorhtme
on rode treo   rodora waldend
æfstum þurh inwit,   swa se ealda feond
forlærde lige-searwum,   leode fortyhte,
Iudea cyn,   þæt hie God sylfne
210 ahengon, herga fruman.   Þæs hie in hynðum sculon
to widan feore   wergðu dreogan.
Þa wæs Cristes lof   þam casere
on firhð-sefan,   forð gemyndig
ymb þæt mære treo,   ond þa his modor het
215 feran fold-wege   folca þreate

Thus wisely in spiritual mysteries they spoke
to the triumphant one, as they had been taught   190
by Sylvester. From them, the leader of the people
received baptism and observed it
the span of his days according to the will of the Lord.

                                                         III

Then the giver of treasure, the bold
king, was happy. A new joy in his heart had been   195
granted him; his greatest of consolations and highest
of hopes was the guardian of the heavenly kingdom.
Day and night, then, through the gift of the Spirit
he started eagerly making known the law of the Lord,
and he, the gold-friend of men, valiant in war, quick,   200
truly applied himself to the service of God.
Then the nobleman,
the people's prince, battle-heard, bold,
found through scholars in the books of God
where the ruler of the firmament had been hanged   205
with hatred on the cross to the acclaim of the army
through guile, as the old enemy
through wiles seduced them, misled the people,
the Jewish race, so that they hanged God
himself, the creator of armies. For that they have to   210
endure banishment forever in humiliations.
Then praise of Christ was in the heart
of the emperor, ever mindful
of that glorious tree, and he commanded his mother
to travel the road with a band of people   215

to Iudeum,   georne secan
wigena þreate   hwær se wuldres beam,
halig under hrusan,   hyded wære,
æðel-cyninges rod.   Elene ne wolde
220 þæs siðfates   sæne weorðan,
ne ðæs wil-gifan   word gehyrwan,
hiere sylfre suna,   ac wæs sona gearu,
wif on will-sið,   swa hire weoruda helm,
byrn-wiggendra,   beboden hæfde.
225 Ongan þa ofstlice   eorla mengu
to flote fysan.   Fearoð-hengestas
ymb geofenes stæð   gearwe stodon,
sælde sæ-mearas,   sunde getenge.
Ða wæs orcnæwe   idese siðfæt,
230 siððan wæges helm   werode gesohte.
Þær wlanc manig   æt Wendel-sæ
on stæðe stodon.   Stundum wræcon
ofer mearc-paðu,   mægen æfter oðrum,
ond þa gehlodon   hilde-sercum,
235 bordum ond ordum,   byrn-wigendum,
werum ond wifum,   wæg-hengestas.
Leton þa ofer fifel-wæg   famige scriðan
bronte brim-þisan.   Bord oft onfeng
ofer earh-geblond   yða swengas;
240 sæ swinsade.   Ne hyrde ic sið ne ær
on eg-streame   idese lædan,
on mere-stræte,   mægen fægerre.
Þær meahte gesion,   se ðone sið beheold,
brecan ofer bæð-weg,   brim-wudu snyrgan

to the Jews, eagerly to seek
with a band of warriors where the tree of glory,
the cross of the noble king, holy under the earth,
might be hidden. Elene would not
be reluctant about that journey,   220
nor despise the word of the gracious ruler,
her own son, but was immediately prepared,
a woman on a gracious errand, to do as the protector of
troops, of warriors in coats of mail, had ordered her.
A crowd of men then began quickly   225
to hasten to the sea. Ships
stood ready along the ocean shore,
sea-mares moored close to the sea.
The journey of the woman was evident,
after she sought the ocean wave with a troop.   230
Many proud men stood there on the shore
of the Mediterranean. At times they pressed forward
over the border roads, one host after another,
and then loaded the wave-horses
with coats of mail, with shields and spears,   235
with warriors, with men and women.
Then they let the steep, foamy ships glide
over the sea. The ship's side often received
the beating of the waves on the ocean flood;
the sea resounded. I have never heard   240
a woman leading a fairer host
on the ocean stream, on the sea-road.
There he who watched the voyage might see
the sea-wood rushing over the waterway, hastening

245 under swellingum,   sæ-mearh plegean,
wadan wæg-flotan.   Wigan wæron bliðe,
collen-ferhðe;   cwen siðes gefeah
syþþan to hyðe   hringed-stefnan
ofer lago-fæsten   geliden hæfdon
250 on Creca land.   Ceolas leton
æt sæ-fearoðe,   sande bewrecene,
ald yð-hofu,   oncrum fæste
on brime bidan   beorna geþinges,
hwonne heo sio guð-cwen   gumena þreate
255 ofer east-wegas   eft gesohte.
Ðær wæs on eorle   eð-gesyne
brogden byrne   ond bill gecost,
geatolic guð-scrud,   grim-helm manig,
ænlic eofor-cumbul.   Wæron æsc-wigan,
260 secggas ymb sige-cwen,   siðes gefysde.
Fyrd-rincas frome   foron on luste
on Creca land,   caseres bodan,
hilde-rincas,   hyrstum gewerede.
Þær wæs gesyne   sinc-gim locen
265 on þam here-þreate,   Hlafordes gifu.
Wæs seo ead-hreðige   Elene gemyndig,
þriste on geþance,   þeodnes willan
georn on mode   þæt hio Iudeas
ofer here-feldas   heape gecoste
270 lind-wigendra   land gesohte,
secga þreate.   Swa hit siððan gelamp
ymb lytel fæc   þæt ðæt leod-mægen,
guð-rofe hæleþ   to Hierusalem

under swelling sails, the sea-mare playing,   245
the wave-floater advancing. The warriors were happy,
bold-spirited; the queen rejoiced in the voyage
after the ring-prowed ships had arrived
at harbor over the water-fastness
in the land of the Greeks. They left the ships,   250
sand beaten, at the seashore,
the old ships fast at anchor
awaiting on the sea the fate of men,
when the war-queen with a troop of men
would seek them again over the eastern paths.   255
There was easily seen on a man
the linked coats of mail and the tried sword,
the magnificent war vestment, many a visored helmet,
the peerless boar-standard. The spear-warriors,
the men around the victory queen, were eager for the   260
journey. The bold army-warriors went with pleasure
into the land of the Greeks, messengers of the emperor,
battle-warriors, clothed in ornaments.
There the treasure-gem was seen set
in that troop, the gift of the Lord.   265
The blessed Elene, bold in thought,
eager in spirit, was mindful of the
will of the prince that she should seek over
battlefields with her tried troop
of shield-warriors, her band of men,   270
the land of the Jews. So it happened
after a little space of time that that host of men,
war-brave heroes, illustrious men, came into the city

cwomon in þa ceastre   corðra mæste,
275 eorlas æsc-rofe,   mid þa æðelan cwen.

IV

Heht ða gebeodan   burg-sittendum
þam snoterestum   side ond wide
geond Iudeas,   gumena gehwylcum,
meðel-hegende,   on gemot cuman,
280 þa ðe deoplicost   Dryhtnes geryno
þurh rihte æ   reccan cuðon.
Ða wæs gesamnod   of sid-wegum
mægen unlytel,   þa ðe Moyses æ
reccan cuðon.   Þær on rime wæs
285 þreo þusendo   þæra leoda
alesen to lare.   Ongan þa leoflic wif
weras Ebrea   wordum negan:
"Ic þæt gearolice   ongiten hæbbe
þurg witgena   word-geryno
290 on Godes bocum   þæt ge gear-dagum
wyrðe wæron   wuldor-cyninge,
Dryhtne dyre   ond dæd-hwæte.
Hwæt, ge þære snyttro   unwislice,
wraðe wiðweorpon,   þa ge wergdon þane
295 þe eow of wergðe   þurh his wuldres miht,
fram lig-cwale,   lysan þohte,
of hæft-nede.   Ge mid horu speowdon
on þæs ondwlitan   þe eow eagena leoht,
fram blindnesse   bote gefremede
300 edniowunga   þurh þæt æðele spald
ond fram unclænum   oft generede
deofla gastum.   Ge deaþe þone
deman ongunnon,   se ðe of deaðe sylf

of Jerusalem with the greatest of companies
with the noble queen.   275

Then she ordered it proclaimed to the wisest
city inhabitants far and wide
among the Jews, to each deliberating man,
to come to a council,
those who most deeply through right law   280
could expound the secrets of the Lord.
Then was gathered from distant lands
a not small host, those who knew how to expound
the law of Moses. There in number were
three thousand of that people   285
selected for instruction. Then the lovely woman began
to address the Hebrew men in words:
"I have completely understood
through the word-secrets of the prophets
in God's books that in former days   290
you were precious to the king of glory,
dear to the Lord and bold.
How foolishly you fiercely
cast away wisdom when you cursed the one
who through his glorious might thought   295
to release you from damnation,
from bondage. With filth you spat
on the face of the one who, with that noble spittle,
worked remedy afresh from blindness
for the light of your eyes   300
and often saved you from the unclean
spirits of devils. You began to condemn to death
the one who himself had in that former

woruld awehte　　on wera corþre

305　in þæt ærre lif　　eowres cynnes.

Swa ge mod-blinde　　mengan ongunnon

lige wið soðe,　　leoht wið þystrum,

æfst wið are,　　inwit-þancum

wroht webbedan.　　Eow seo wergðu forðan

310　sceðþeð scyldfullum.　　Ge þa sciran miht

deman ongunnon　　ond gedweolan lifdon,

þeostrum geþancum,　　oð þysne dæg.

Gangaþ nu snude,　　snyttro geþencaþ,

weras wisfæste,　　wordes cræftige,

315　þa ðe eowre æ　　æðelum cræftige

on ferhð-sefan　　fyrmest hæbben,

þa me soðlice　　secgan cunnon,

ondsware cyðan　　for eowic forð

tacna gehwylces　　þe ic him to sece.”

320　Eodan þa on gerum　　reonig-mode

eorlas æ-cleawe,　　egesan geþreade,

gehðum geomre,　　georne sohton

þa wisestan　　word-geryno,

þæt hio þære cwene　　oncweðan meahton

325　swa tiles swa trages,　　swa hio him to sohte.

Hio þa on þreate　　þusendo manna

fundon ferhð-gleawra,　　þa þe fyrn-gemynd

mid Iudeum　　gearwast cuðon.

Þrungon þa on þreate　　þær on þrymme bad

330　in cyne-stole　　caseres mæg,

geatolic guð-cwen　　golde gehyrsted.

Elene maþelode　　ond for eorlum spræc:

“Gehyrað, hige-gleawe,　　halige rune,

life raised up the world from death among the people
of your race in the company of men.   305
Thus spiritually blind you began to confound
lying with truth, light with darkness,
envy with mercy, to contrive
slander with malice. Therefore, damnation will harm you
sinful ones. You began to condemn   310
the bright power and have lived in error,
with dark thoughts, until this day.
Go now quickly, wise men, skilled in words,
with wisdom consider
those who, skilled in lineage,   315
most firmly have your law in their minds,
those who can truly tell me,
reveal to me before you, the answer
I seek from them for every remarkable event."
Sorrowful they went away then,   320
the men skilled in law, tormented with fear,
troubled with anxieties, eagerly sought
the wisest word-secrets
so that they might answer the queen,
for good or for ill, as she inquired of them.   325
They then found in a troop a thousand
wise men, those who among the Jews most readily knew
the memory of former times.
They thronged in a troop then to where the kinswoman
of the emperor waited in glory on a royal   330
throne, the magnificent battle-queen adorned with gold.
Elene made a formal speech and spoke before the men:
"Listen, wise men, to the holy secret,

word ond wisdom.   Hwæt, ge witgena
335   lare onfengon,   hu se Lif-Fruma
in cildes had   cenned wurde,
mihta wealdend.   Be þam Moyses sang,
ond þæt word gecwæð   weard Israhela:
'Eow acenned bið   cniht on degle,
340   mihtum mære,   swa þæs modor ne bið
wæstmum geeacnod   þurh weres frige.'
Be ðam Dauid cyning   dryht-leoð agol,
frod fyrn-weota,   fæder Salomones,
ond þæt word gecwæþ   wigona baldor:
345   'Ic frumþa God   fore sceawode,
sigora Dryhten.   He on gesyhðe wæs,
mægena wealdend,   min on þa swiðran,
þrymmes hyrde.   Þanon ic ne wendo
æfre to aldre   onsion mine.'
350   Swa hit eft be eow   Essaias,
witga for weorodum,   wordum mælde,
deop-hycggende   þurh Dryhtnes gast:
'Ic up ahof   eaforan gingne
ond bearn cende,   þam ic blæd forgeaf,
355   halige hige-frofre,   ac hie hyrwdon me,
feodon þurh feondscipe,   nahton fore-þances,
wisdomes gewitt;   ond þa weregan neat
þe man daga gehwam   drifeð ond þirsceð,
ongitaþ hira god-dend,   nales gnyrn-wræcum
360   feogað frynd hiera   þe him fodder gifað,
ond me Israhela   æfre ne woldon

to my words and wisdom. Yes, you have received
the teaching of the prophets, how the Lord of life,   335
the ruler of might, was born in the form
of a child. About him Moses the guardian
of the Israelites, sang and spoke these words:
'A boy will be born to you in secret,
glorious in might, whose mother will not be   340
increased with child through a man's love.'
About him King David chanted a heroic song,
the wise sage, the father of Solomon,
the leader of warriors, and spoke these words:
'I have foreseen the God of beginnings,   345
the Lord of victories. He, the ruler of hosts,
the guardian of glory, was in my sight,
on my right hand. I shall not
turn my face from there.'
Thus afterward about you Isaiah, the prophet,   350
deep-thinking through the spirit of the Lord,
spoke in words before the people:
'I have raised up a young son
and begotten child, to whom I gave prosperity,
holy consolation of mind, but they despised me,   355
hated me through enmity, did not have understanding
of forethought, of wisdom; and the weary oxen
that someone drives and beats every day,
recognize their benefactors, not at all in vengeance
for grief hate their friends who give them fodder,   360
and the people of Israel never

folc oncnawan,   þeah ic feala for him
æfter woruld-stundum   wundra gefremede.'

v

"Hwæt, we þæt gehyrdon   þurh halige bec
365   þæt eow Dryhten geaf   dom unscyndne,
meotod mihta sped,   Moyse sægde
hu ge heofon-cyninge   hyran sceoldon,
lare læstan.   Eow þæs lungre aþreat,
ond ge þam ryhte   wiðroten hæfdon,
370   onscunedon þone sciran   scippend, eallra Dryhten,
ond gedwolan fylgdon
ofer riht Godes.   Nu ge raþe gangaþ
ond findaþ gen   þa þe fyrn-gewritu
þurh snyttro cræft   selest cunnen,
375   æ-riht eower,   þæt me ondsware
þurh sidne sefan   secgan cunnen."
Eodan ða mid mengo   mod-cwanige,
collen-ferhðe,   swa him sio cwen bead.
Fundon þa fifhund   forþ-snottera
380   alesen leod-mæga,   þa ðe leornung-cræft
þurh mod-gemynd   mæste hæfdon,
on sefan snyttro.   Heo to salore eft
ymb lytel fæc   laðode wæron,
ceastre weardas.   Hio sio cwen ongan
385   wordum genegan,   —wlat ofer ealle:
"Oft ge dyslice   dæd gefremedon,
werge wræc-mæcggas,   ond gewritu herwdon,
fædera lare,   næfre furður þonne nu,
ða ge blindnesse   bote forsegon,
390   ond ge wiðsocon   soðe ond rihte,

wanted to recognize me, although I
worked many a wonder for them in the world.'

v

"How much we have heard through holy books
that the Lord, the creator, gave you unblemished fame,   365
abundance of power, said to Moses
that you should obey the heavenly king,
perform his teaching. This became irksome to you right
away, and you have opposed that law,
shunned the bright creator, Lord of all,   370
and followed delusion
contrary to the law of God. Now go quickly
and find again those who know best the ancient writings,
your law, through skillful wisdom
so that through broad intellect   375
they might give an answer to me."
Then the ones sorrowful in spirit, proud in heart,
went away in a multitude as the queen had commanded.
They found 500 of the very wise ones
selected from their people who had the most   380
skill of learning through intelligence,
wisdom in their minds. They, the guardians of the city,
were invited to the hall again
after a little while. The queen began
to address them in words—she peered over all of them: 385
"Often you, wretched outcasts, have done
a foolish deed and despised the scriptures,
the teaching of your fathers, never more than now,
when you rejected the remedy for blindness,
and you denied truth and right,   390

169

þæt in Bethleme   Bearn wealdendes,
cyning anboren,   cenned wære,
æðelinga ord.   Þeah ge þa æ cuðon,
witgena word,   ge ne woldon þa,
395   syn-wyrcende,   soð oncnawan."
Hie þa an-mode   ondsweredon:
"Hwæt, we Ebreisce   æ leornedon,
þa on fyrn-dagum   fæderas cuðon
æt Godes earce;   ne we geare cunnon
400   þurh hwæt ðu ðus hearde,   hlæfdige, us
eorre wurde.   We ðæt æbylgð nyton
þe we gefremedon   on þysse folc-scere,
þeoden-bealwa,   wið þec æfre."
Elene maðelade   ond for eorlum spræc,
405   undearninga   ides reordode
hlude for herigum: "Ge nu hraðe gangað,
sundor asecaþ   þa ðe snyttro mid eow,
mægn ond mod-cræft,   mæste hæbben,
þæt me þinga gehwylc   þriste gecyðan,
410   untraglice,   þe ic him to sece."
Eodon þa fram rune,   swa him sio rice cwen,
bald in burgum,   beboden hæfde,
geomor-mode,   georne smeadon,
sohton searo-þancum,   hwæt sio syn wære
415   þe hie on þam folce   gefremed hæfdon
wið þam casere,   þe him sio cwen wite.
Þa þær for eorlum   an reordode,
gidda gearo-snotor,   —ðam wæs Iudas nama,
wordes cræftig: "Ic wat geare

that in Bethlehem the Son of the ruler,
the only-begotten king, the prince of nobles,
was born. Although you knew the law,
the words of the prophets, you, sinful ones,
would not recognize the truth."   395
In accord, they all then answered:
"Yes, we learned the Hebrew law,
which in days past our fathers knew
at the ark of God; we do not fully understand
why you, lady, have become so severely angry   400
with us. We do not know the transgression,
the terrible evils, that we have ever committed
in this nation against you."
Elene made a formal speech, spoke before the men,
plainly and loudly the woman made her voice   405
heard before the troops: "Go now quickly,
seek out those among you who have
most wisdom, strength, and intelligence,
so that they may boldly, honestly, make known
to me what I seek from them."   410
Mournful in mind, they departed then from council
as the powerful queen, bold in the cities, had
commanded them, earnestly considered,
sought through subtle thoughts, what the sin might be
that the queen accused them of that they   415
had committed against the emperor among the people.
Then before the men there one,
exceedingly wise of songs—whose name was Judas,
skilled in words—spoke up: "I know well

420 þæt hio wile secan   be ðam sige-beame
on ðam þrowode   þeoda waldend,
eallra gnyrna leas,   Godes agen bearn,
þone orscyldne   eofota gehwylces
þurh hete hengon   on heanne beam
425 in fyrn-dagum   fæderas usse.
    Þæt wæs þrealic geþoht.   Nu is þearf mycel
þæt we fæstlice   ferhð staðelien,
þæt we ðæs morðres   meldan ne weorðen
hwær þæt halige trio   beheled wurde
430 æfter wig-þræce,   þy læs toworpen sien
frod fyrn-gewritu   ond þa fæderlican
lare forleten.   Ne bið lang ofer ðæt
þæt Israhela   æðelu moten
ofer middan-geard   ma ricsian,
435 æ-cræft eorla,   gif ðis yppe bið.
    Swa þa þæt ilce gio   min yldra fæder
sige-rof sægde   —þam wæs Sachius nama—
frod fyrn-wiota,   fæder minum,
    . . .   eaferan;
440 wende hine of worulde   ond þæt word gecwæð:
'Gif þe þæt gelimpe   on lif-dagum
þæt ðu gehyre   ymb þæt halige treo
frode frignan,   ond geflitu ræran
be ðam sige-beame   on þam soð-cyning
445 ahangen wæs,   heofon-rices weard,
eallre sybbe bearn,   þonne þu snude gecyð,
min swæs sunu,   ær þec swylt nime.
    Ne mæg æfre ofer þæt   Ebrea þeod
ræd-þeahtende   rice healdan,
450 duguðum wealdan,   ac þara dom leofað

that she wants to ask about the tree of victory   420
on which the ruler of peoples suffered,
free of all sins,
God's own child, guiltless of each of crimes,
whom our fathers in days gone by
through hatred hanged on the high tree.   425
That was a terrible idea. Now the need is great
that we set our hearts firmly
so that we do not become informers
about the murder nor where that holy tree was hidden
after the strife, lest the wise ancient records   430
should be destroyed and the teachings of our fathers
abandoned. If this became known,
it would not be long after that that the nobles of Israel,
the religion of our people, might rule in
middle-earth any more.   435
So that same thing long ago my
triumphant grandfather—his name was Zachaeus—
the wise prophet, said to my father,
...   to his son;
he turned from the world and spoke these words: 440
'If it should happen to you in the days of your life
that you should hear wise men ask
and raise dispute about the holy tree,
about the tree of victory on which the true king,
the guardian of the heavenly kingdom,   445
the child of all peace, was hanged, then, my dear son,
speak quickly before death should take you.
After that the wise Hebrew people
can never hold the kingdom,
rule men, but the fame and authority of those   450

173

ond hira dryhtscipe,
in woruld weorulda   willum gefylled,
ðe þone ahangnan cyning   heriaþ ond lofiað.'

"Þa ic fromlice   fæder minum,
455 ealdum æ-witan,   ageaf ondsware:
'Hu wolde þæt geweorðan   on woruld-rice
þæt on þone halgan   handa sendan
to feorh-lege   fæderas usse
þurh wrað gewitt,   gif hie wiston ær
460 þæt he Crist wære,   cyning on roderum,
soð Sunu meotudes,   sawla nergend?'
Ða me yldra min   ageaf ondsware;
frod on fyrhðe   fæder reordode:
'Ongit, guma ginga,   Godes heah-mægen,
465 nergendes naman.   Se is niða gehwam
unasecgendlic,   þone sylf ne mæg
on mold-wege   man aspyrigean.
Næfre ic þa geþeahte   þe þeos þeod ongan
secan wolde,   ac ic symle mec
470 asced þara scylda,   nales sceame worhte
gaste minum.   Ic him georne oft
þæs unrihtes   ondsæc fremede,
þonne uðweotan   æht bisæton,
on sefan sohton   hu hie Sunu meotudes
475 ahengon, helm wera,   Hlaford eallra
engla ond elda,   æðelust bearna.
Ne meahton hie swa disige   deað oðfæstan,
weras won-sælige,   swa hie wendon ær,
sarum settan,   þeah he sume hwile

who, filled with joy,
honor and praise the crucified king
will live forever and ever.'

"Then boldly I gave answer to my father,
the old counselor: 455
'How would that happen in the worldly kingdom
that our fathers by their own hand
should send the holy one to death
through hostile understanding if they knew beforehand
that he was Christ, the king of the firmament,   460
the true Son of the creator, the savior of souls?'
Then my parent gave me an answer;
wise in heart my father spoke:
'Understand, young man, God's great power,
the savior's name. For everyone, he is   465
ineffable whom no one can discover
on the earth.
I never wanted to seek the counsel
that this people undertook, but I always kept myself
separate from those crimes, did not at all bring shame   470
on my soul. I often eagerly
opposed them for that injustice,
when the wise men held counsel,
looked in their hearts for how they could crucify
the Son of the creator, the protector of men,   475
the Lord of all angels and people, noblest of children.
Such foolish, accursed men could not
inflict death, as they had expected they could,
beset him with wounds, although after a while

480   on galgan his   gast onsende,
      sige-bearn Godes.   Þa siððan wæs
      of rode ahæfen   rodera wealdend,
      eallra þrymma þrym,   þreo-niht siððan
      in byrgenne   bidende wæs
485   under þeoster-locan,   ond þa þy þriddan dæg
      ealles leohtes leoht   lifgende aras,
      ðeoden engla,   ond his þegnum,
      soð sigora Frea,   seolfne geywde,
      beorht on blæde.   Þonne broðor þin
490   onfeng æfter fyrste   fulwihtes bæð,
      leohtne geleafan.   Þa for lufan Dryhtnes
      Stephanus wæs   stanum worpod;
      ne geald he yfel yfele,   ac his eald-feondum
      þingode þroht-herd,   bæd þrym-cyning
495   þæt he him þa wea-dæd   to wræce ne sette,
      þæt hie for æfstum   unscyldigne,
      synna leasne,   Sawles larum
      feore beræddon,   swa he þurh feondscipe
      to cwale monige   Cristes folces
500   demde to deaþe.   Swa þeah him Dryhten eft
      miltse gefremede,   þæt he manegum wearð
      folca to frofre,   syððan him frymða God,
      niða nergend,   naman oncyrde,
      ond he syððan wæs   sanctus Paulus
505   be naman haten,   ond him nænig wæs
      æ-lærendra   oðer betera
      under swegles hleo   syðþan æfre,
      þara þe wif oððe wer   on woruld cendan,

on the cross he, the victorious child of God,   480
sent forth his soul. Then afterward
the ruler of the heavens, the glory of all glories,
was lifted down from the rood; three nights later
he was waiting in the tomb
in the dark chamber, and on the third day   485
the light of all light,
the prince of angels, arose alive and
the true Lord of victories showed himself,
bright in joy, to his disciples. Then after a time
your brother received the bath of baptism,   490
the bright faith. Then for his love of the Lord,
Stephen was stoned;
he did not repay evil with evil, but for his old enemies
the patient one interceded, prayed to the king of glory
that he should not avenge on them that sorrow-bringing   495
deed that they for envy deprived the guiltless one,
the one without sin, of life through the teachings
of Saul, just as he through enmity
had condemned many of Christ's people to murder
and death. Yet the Lord showed him   500
mercy afterward, so that to many of the people
he became a consolation, since the God of beginnings,
the savior of men, changed his name,
and he afterward was called Saint Paul
by name, and there was none other of law teachers   505
better than he under the
protection of the sky for ever after,
of those who woman or man engendered in the world,

þeah he Stephanus   stanum hehte
510   abreotan on beorge,   broðor þinne.
Nu ðu meaht gehyran,   hæleð min se leofa,
hu arfæst is   ealles wealdend,
þeah we æbylgð wið hine   oft gewyrcen,
synna wunde,   gif we sona eft
515   þara bealu-dæda   bote gefremmaþ
ond þæs unrihtes   eft geswicaþ.
Forðan ic soðlice   ond min swæs fæder
syðþan gelyfdon
þæt geþrowade   eallra þrymma God,
520   lifes lattiow,   laðlic wite
for ofer-þearfe   ilda cynnes.
Forðan ic þe lære   þurh leoðo-rune,
hyse leofesta,   þæt ðu hosp-cwide,
æfst ne eoful-sæc   æfre ne fremme,
525   grimne geagn-cwide,   wið Godes Bearne.
Þonne ðu geearnast   þæt þe bið ece lif,
selust sige-leana,   seald in heofonum.'
Ðus mec fæder min   on fyrn-dagum
unweaxenne   wordum lærde,
530   septe soð-cwidum;   þam wæs Symon nama,
guma gehðum frod.   Nu ge geare cunnon
hwæt eow þæs on sefan   selest þince
to gecyðanne,   gif ðeos cwen usic
frigneð ymb ðæt treo,   nu ge fyrhð-sefan
535   ond mod-geþanc   minne cunnon."
Him þa togenes   þa gleawestan
on wera þreate   wordum mældon:
"Næfre we hyrdon   hæleð ænigne

178

even though he ordered Stephen, your brother,
slain with stones on the mountain.   510
Now you can hear, my beloved man,
how gracious the ruler of all is,
although we often transgress against him,
wound him with sins, if we will immediately afterward
repent the evil deeds   515
and desist from wrong.
Therefore I and my dear father truly
believed afterward
that the God of all glories,
the leader of life, had suffered loathsome torment   520
because of the great need of the human race.
Therefore, I instruct you through wise counsel,
dearest youth, that you should never express
blasphemy, envy, or slander,
grim answer, against the Son of God.   525
Then you will deserve that eternal life, the best
of victory rewards, will be given to you in
        heaven.'
Thus my father in ancient days
when I was young taught me in words,
instructed me with true sayings; his name was Simon,   530
a man wise in sorrows. Now you clearly know
what seems best to you in your heart
to make known, if this queen
asks us about that tree, now that you know
my mind and thought."   535
To him then the wisest
in the throng of men spoke in words:
"We have never heard any man

179

on þysse þeode,   butan þec nuða,
540   þegn oðerne   þyslic cyðan
ymb swa dygle wyrd.   Do swa þe þynce,
fyrn-gidda frod,   gif ðu frugnen sie
on wera corðre.   Wisdomes beðearf,
worda wærlicra   ond witan snyttro,
545   se ðære æðelan sceal   ondwyrde agifan
for þyslicne   þreat on meþle."

VII

Weoxan word cwidum,   weras þeahtedon
on healfa gehwær,   sume hyder, sume þyder,
þrydedon ond þohton.   Þa cwom þegna heap
550   to þam here-meðle.   Hreopon friccan,
caseres bodan: "Eow þeos cwen laþaþ,
secgas to salore,   þæt ge seonoð-domas
rihte reccen.   Is eow rædes þearf
on meðel-stede,   modes snyttro."
555   Heo wæron gearwe,   geomor-mode
leod-gebyrgean,   þa hie laðod wæron
þurh heard gebann;   to hofe eodon,
cyðdon cræftes miht.   Þa sio cwen ongan
weras Ebresce   wordum negan,
560   fricggan fyrhð-werige   ymb fyrn-gewritu,
hu on worulde ær   witgan sungon,
gast-halige guman,   be Godes bearne,
hwær se þeoden   geþrowade,
soð Sunu meotudes,   for sawla lufan.
565   Heo wæron stearce,   stane heardran,

from this nation, except you just now,
any other attendant, speak thus   540
about so secret an event. Do what seems best to you,
wise in ancient lore, if you should be questioned
in the company of men. He has need of wisdom,
of cunning words and of the sagacity of a wiseman,
he who must give answer to the noble woman   545
in council before this troop."

VII

Words grew into speeches, men took counsel
on both sides, some here, some there,
deliberating and thinking. Then a troop of attendants
came to the assembly. Heralds called out,   550
the messengers of the emperor: "The queen invites you
men to the hall so that you may rightly relate
the assembly's decrees. There is a need of counsel from
you in the assembly place, the wisdom of your mind."
They were ready, the sorrowful   555
princes, when they were invited
through the hard command; they went to the court,
showed the might of their knowledge. Then the queen
began to address in words the Hebrew men,
ask the heart-weary ones about ancient records,   560
how wise men sang in the world before,
men holy in spirit, about the child of God,
where the prince suffered,
the true Son of the creator, for the love of souls.
They, her bitter foes, were obstinate, harder than stone,   565

noldon þæt geryne   rihte cyðan,
ne hire andsware   ænige secgan,
torn-geniðlan,   þæs hio him to sohte,
ac hio worda gehwæs   wiðer-sæc fremedon,
570 fæste on fyrhðe,   þæt heo frignan ongan,
cwædon þæt hio on aldre   owiht swylces
ne ær ne sið   æfre hyrdon.
Elene maþelade   ond him yrre oncwæð:
"Ic eow to soðe   secgan wille,
575 ond þæs in life   lige ne wyrðeð,
gif ge þissum lease   leng gefylgað
mid fæcne gefice,   þe me fore standaþ,
þæt eow in beorge   bæl fornimeð,
hattost heaðo-welma,   ond eower hra bryttað,
580 lacende lig,   þæt eow sceal þæt leas
apundrad weorðan   to woruld-gedale.
Ne magon ge ða word geseðan   þe ge hwile nu on unriht
wrigon under womma sceatum,   ne magon ge þa wyrd
                                    bemiðan,
bedyrnan þa deopan mihte."   Ða wurdon hie deaðes on
                                    wenan,
585 ades ond ende-lifes,   ond þær þa ænne betæhton
giddum gearu-snottorne,   þam wæs Iudas nama
cenned for cneo-magum;   þone hie þære cwene agefon,
sægdon hine sundor-wisne: "He þe mæg soð gecyðan,
onwreon wyrda geryno,   swa ðu hine wordum frignest,
590 æ-riht from orde   oð ende forð.
He is for eorðan   æðeles cynnes,

did not want rightly to reveal that secret
nor give any answer to her
about what she sought from them,
but they resisted each of her words,
firm in heart, so that she began to ask,   570
they said that they had never in their life
had heard of any such thing.
Angry, Elene made a formal speech and said to them:
"I will tell you in truth,
and on my life, this is not a lie,   575
if you who stand before me persist longer
in these falsehoods with old deceit,
that a pyre, the hottest of fierce flames,
will consume you on the hill, and the leaping fire
will destroy your corpses because that lie will be   580
accounted in you worthy of death. You cannot prove
those words true which you for a while now wrongly
concealed in the corners of your sins, nor can you hide
        the event,
obscure the deep power." Then they expected death,
the pyre, and the end of life, and handed over there one   585
very wise in songs who was known to his kinsmen
by the name Judas; they gave him to the queen,
called him singularly wise: "He can reveal the truth to
you, disclose the mystery of events, the law from
the beginning to the end as you ask him to do.   590
He is of noble kindred in the world,

word-cræftes wis ond witgan sunu,
bald on meðle; him gebyrde is
þæt he gen-cwidas gleawe hæbbe,
595 cræft in breostum. He gecyðeð þe
for wera mengo wisdomes gife
þurh þa myclan miht, swa þin mod lufaþ."
Hio on sybbe forlet secan gehwylcne
agenne eard, ond þone ænne genam,
600 Iudas to gisle, ond þa georne bæd
þæt he be ðære rode riht getæhte
þe ær in legere wæs lange bedyrned,
ond hine seolfne sundor acigde.
Elene maþelode to þam an-hagan,
605 tir-eadig cwen: "Þe synt tu gearu,
swa lif swa deað, swa þe leofre bið
to geceosanne. Cyð ricene nu
hwæt ðu þæs to þinge þafian wille."
Iudas hire ongen þingode (ne meahte he þa gehðu
bebugan,
610 oncyrran rex geniðlan; he wæs on þære cwene
gewealdum):
"Hu mæg þæm geweorðan þe on westenne
meðe ond meteleas mor-land trydeð,
hungre gehæfted, ond him hlaf ond stan
on gesihðe bu samod geweorðað,
615 streac ond hnesce, þæt he þone stan nime
wið hungres hleo, hlafes ne gime,

wise in word-craft and the son of a prophet,
bold in council; it is innate in him
that he should have wise answers,
skill in his heart. He will reveal to you   595
before the multitude of men the gift of wisdom
through his great power, as your heart desires."
She let each in the tribe to go in peace to
his own dwelling and took just the one,
Judas, hostage and then eagerly asked   600
him to tell the truth about the cross,
which had been long hidden until then
in its resting place, and she took him aside.
Elene, the glorious queen, made a formal speech
to the solitary man: "For you, two things are prepared,   605
either life or death, whatever is dearer to you
for the choosing. Make known quickly now
what you want." Judas spoke to her
(he could not escape anxiety, nor could the king
change that torment; he was in the queen's power):   610
"How can that happen for the one weary and without
food in the wilderness who treads the moorland,
oppressed with hunger, and for whom both bread and
    stone,
the hard and the soft, both appear together to his vision,
that he should take the stone   615
for refuge against hunger and heed not the bread,

gewende to wædle,   ond þa wiste wiðsæce,
beteran wiðhyccge,   þonne he bega beneah?"

Him þa seo eadige   ondwyrde ageaf

620   Elene for eorlum   undearnunga:
"Gif ðu in heofon-rice   habban wille
eard mid englum   ond on eorðan lif,
sigor-lean in swegle,   saga ricene me
hwær seo rod wunige   rador-cyninges,

625   halig under hrusan,   þe ge hwile nu
þurh morðres man   mannum dyrndun."
Iudas maðelade,   —him wæs geomor sefa,
hat æt heortan,   ond gehwæðres wa;
ge him heofon-rices   hyht swamode

630   ond þis ondwearde   anforlete,
rice under roderum,   ge he ða rode getæhte:
"Hu mæg ic þæt findan   þæt swa fyrn gewearð
wintra gangum?   Is nu worn sceacen,
tu hund oððe ma   geteled rime.

635   Ic ne mæg areccan,   nu ic þæt rim ne can.
Is nu feala siðþan   forð-gewitenra
frodra ond godra   þe us fore wæron,
gleawra gumena.   Ic on geogoðe wearð
on sið-dagum   syððan acenned,

640   cniht-geong hæleð.   Ic ne can þæt ic nat
findan on fyrhðe   þæt swa fyrn gewearð."
Elene maðelade   him on ondsware:
"Hu is þæt geworden   on þysse wer-þeode
þæt ge swa monigfeald   on gemynd witon,

turn to want and refuse the food,
scorn the better when he has both at his disposal?"

The blessed Elene then answered him
plainly before the people: 620
"If you wish to have in heaven
an abode with the angels and life on earth,
reward of victory in the sky, tell me quickly
where the cross of the king of heaven might rest,
holy under the ground, which you for a while now   625
through the sin of murder have concealed from humans."
Judas made a formal speech—his spirit was sad,
hot around the heart, and there was woe for each of two
          things;
the hope of the heavenly kingdom growing dim for him
and he would have to leave the present, the kindgom   630
under the firmament, and revealing the cross:
"How can I find that which happened so long ago
in the course of winters? A great many have now passed,
200 or more reckoned in numbers.
I cannot tell now, since I do not know that number.   635
Now many wise and good and
sagacious men who came before us
have passed away. I, as a young man,
was born into youth after them
in later days. I cannot find in my heart   640
what I do not know, what happened so long ago."
Elene made a formal speech in answer to him:
"How can it be in this nation
that you keep in memory so many things,

645　alra tacna gehwylc　swa Troiana
þurh gefeoht fremedon?　Þæt wæs fyr mycle,
open eald-gewin,　þonne þeos æðele gewyrd,
geara gongum.　Ge þæt geare cunnon
edre gereccan,　hwæt þær eallra wæs
650　on man-rime　morðor-slehtes,
dareð-lacendra　deadra gefeallen
under bord-hagan.　Ge þa byrgenna
under stan-hleoðum,　ond þa stowe swa some,
ond þa winter-gerim　on gewritu setton."
655　Iudas maðelade,　gnorn-sorge wæg:
"We þæs here-weorces,　hlæfdige min,
for nyd-þearfe　nean myndgiaþ,
ond þa wigg-þræce　on gewritu setton,
þeoda gebæru,　ond þis næfre
660　þurh æniges mannes　muð gehyrdon
hæleðum cyðan,　butan her nuða."
Him seo æðele cwen　ageaf ondsware:
"Wiðsæcest ðu to swiðe　soðe ond rihte
ymb þæt lifes treow,　ond nu lytle ær
665　sægdest soðlice　be þam sige-beame
leodum þinum,　ond nu on lige cyrrest."
Iudas hire ongen þingode,　cwæð þæt he þæt on gehðu
gespræce
ond on tweon swiðost,　wende him trage hnagre.
Him oncwæð hraðe　caseres mæg:
670　"Hwæt, we ðæt hyrdon　þurh halige bec
hæleðum cyðan　þæt ahangen wæs
on Caluarie　cyninges Freo-Bearn,

each of all the wonders that the Trojans   645
accomplished through war? That ancient, famous battle
was much longer ago in the passage of time
than this noble event. You readily know how
to recount immediately what slaughter there was
in the total number of men,   650
of spear-playing ones, of the fallen dead
behind the shield-wall. You must have recorded in
writing the tomb under the cliffs and the place as well
and the number of winters."
Judas made a speech, feeling grief: 655
"We, my lady, necessarily remember
that warfare clearly
and have set down the battle, the acts
of nations, in writing, but we have never
heard this revealed from anyone's mouth   660
until here just now."
The noble woman gave him answer:
"You deny too quickly the truth and right
about the tree of life, yet a little earlier now
you spoke truthfully about the victory tree   665
to your people, and now you turn to lying."
Judas argued against her, saying that he said what he had
          in anxiety
and in the greatest doubt, expecting humiliating afflic-
          tion for himself.
The emperor's kinswoman spoke quickly to him:
"Listen, we have heard made known   670
through holy books that
the noble child of the king, the spiritual Son of God

Godes gast-sunu.   Þu scealt geagninga
wisdom onwreon,   swa gewritu secgaþ,
675 æfter stede-wange   hwær seo stow sie
Caluarie   ær þec cwealm nime,
swilt for synnum,   þæt ic hie syððan mæge
geclænsian   Criste to willan,
hæleðum to helpe,   þæt me halig God
680 gefylle, Frea mihtig,   feores in-geþanc,
weoruda wuldor-geofa,   willan minne,
gasta geocend."   Hire Iudas oncwæð
stið-hycgende: "Ic þa stowe ne can,
ne þæs wanges wiht   ne þa wisan cann."
685 Elene maðelode   þurh eorne hyge:
"Ic þæt geswerige   þurh Sunu meotodes,
þone ahangnan god,   þæt ðu hungre scealt
for cneo-magum   cwylmed weorðan,
butan þu forlæte   þa leasunga
690 ond me sweotollice   soð gecyðe."
Heht þa swa cwicne   corðre lædan,
scufan scyldigne   — scealcas ne gældon—
in drygne seað,   þær he duguða leas
siomode in sorgum   seofon-nihta fyrst
695 under hearm-locan   hungre geþreatod,
clommum beclungen,   ond þa cleopigan ongan
sarum besylced   on þone seofeðan dæg,
meðe ond meteleas,   —mægen wæs geswiðrod:
"Ic eow healsie   þurh heofona God
700 þæt ge me of ðyssum earfeðum   up forlæten,
heanne fram hungres geniðlan.   Ic þæt halige treo

190

was hanged on Calvary. You must completely
disclose the wisdom, as the writings tell us,
about the place Calvary where the tree   675
might be before killing takes you,
death for your sins, so that I may afterward
cleanse it according to Christ's will,
as a help for human beings, so that holy God,
the mighty Lord, the giver of glory of hosts,   680
the helper of spirits may fulfill my purpose, my will,
from long ago." To her the resolute
Judas said: "I do not know that place, nor anything
about the site, nor do I know the direction."
Elene made a speech with an eager heart: 685
"I swear by the Son of the creator,
the crucified god, that you will
be killed by starvation in front of your kinsmen,
unless you put aside those lies
and clearly make known the truth to me."   690
She then ordered him led away alive by a company
and the guilty one pushed—the servants did not
hesitate—into a dry pit where, lacking retinue,
he abided in sorrow for the space of seven nights,
tormented in prison by hunger,   695
bound with fetters, and then on the seventh day,
exhausted with wounds, weary and without food
—his strength was diminished—began to call out:
"I beseech you by the God of the heavens
that from these tortures you should loose me,   700
wretched from the torment of hunger. I

lustum cyðe,　nu ic hit leng ne mæg
helan for hungre.　Is þes hæft to ðan strang,
þrea-nyd þæs þearl　ond þes þroht to ðæs heard
705　dogor-rimum.　Ic adreogan ne mæg,
ne leng helan　be ðam lifes treo,
þeah ic ær mid dysige　þurhdrifen wære
ond ðæt soð to late　seolf gecneowe."

IX

Þa ðæt gehyrde　sio þær hæleðum scead,
710　beornes gebæro,　hio bebead hraðe
þæt hine man of nearwe　ond of nyd-cleofan,
fram þam engan hofe　up forlete.
Hie ðæt ofstlice　efnedon sona,
ond hine mid arum　up gelæddon
715　of carcerne,　swa him seo cwen bebead.
Stopon þa to þære stowe　stið-hycgende
on þa dune up　ðe Dryhten ær
ahangen wæs,　heofon-rices weard,
God-Bearn on galgan,　ond hwæðre geare nyste,
720　hungre gehyned,　hwær sio halige rod,
þurh feondes searu　foldan getyned,
lange legere fæst　leodum dyrne
wunode wæl-reste.　Word stunde ahof
elnes oncyðig,　ond on Ebrisc spræc:
725　"Dryhten hælend,　þu ðe ahst doma geweald,
ond þu geworhtest　þurh þines wuldres miht
heofon ond eorðan　ond holm-þræce,
sæs sidne fæðm,　samod ealle gesceaft,

will gladly make known that holy tree, now that I can no
longer hide it because of hunger. This captivity is
too strong, the cruel necessity too severe and this
affliction too hard in this series of days I cannot endure   705
nor longer conceal the tree of life,
although earlier I was permeated with folly
and too late knew that truth for myself."

IX

When she who ruled over the people there heard that,
the bearing of the man, she immediately ordered   710
that they should let him come up out of imprisonment
and from confinement, from the narrow house.
They quickly and immediately did that
and mercifully led him up
from incarceration, as the queen had ordered.   715
Then, resolute, they walked to the place
up on the hill where the Lord,
the guardian of the heavenly kingdom, had been hanged,
the divine Son on the gallows, and yet, humbled by
hunger, he did not clearly know where the holy cross,   720
enclosed in the earth through the cunning of the enemy,
long fast in its bed, hidden secret from the people,
dwelled in its place of rest on the battlefield. Revealing
    courage,
he raised up words at once and spoke in Hebrew:
"Lord savior, you who hold power over judgments,   725
you made through the might of your glory
heaven and earth and the stormy sea,
the wide bosom of the deep, together with all creation,

ond þu amæte   mundum þinum
730   ealne ymb-hwyrft   ond up-rador,
ond þu sylf sitest,   sigora waldend,
ofer þam æðelestan   engel-cynne,
þe geond lyft farað   leohte bewundene,
mycle mægen-þrymme.   Ne mæg þær manna gecynd
735   of eorð-wegum   up geferan
in lic-homan   mid þa leohtan gedryht,
wuldres aras.   Þu geworhtest þa
ond to þegnunge   þinre gesettest,
halig ond heofonlic.   Þara on hade sint
740   in sindreame   syx genemned,
þa ymbsealde synt   mid syxum eac
fiðrum gefrætwad,   fægere scinaþ.
Þara sint feower   þe on flihte a
þa þegnunge   þrymme beweotigaþ
745   fore onsyne   eces deman,
singallice   singaþ in wuldre
hædrum stefnum   heofon-cininges lof,
woða wlite-gaste,   ond þas word cweðaþ
clænum stefnum,   —þam is ceruphin nama:
750   'Halig is se halga   heah-engla God,
weoroda wealdend!   Is ðæs wuldres ful
heofun ond eorðe   ond eall heah-mægen,
tire getacnod.'   Syndon tu on þam,
sigor-cynn on swegle,   þe man seraphin
755   be naman hateð.   He sceal neorxnawang
ond lifes treo   legene sweorde
halig healdan.   Heard-ecg cwacaþ,
beofaþ brogden-mæl,   ond bleom wrixleð
grapum gryre-fæst.   Þæs ðu, God Dryhten,

and measured with your hands
all the orb and firmament,   730
and yourself sit, ruler of victories,
over the most noble race of angels,
who throughout the air travel surrounded by light,
by great majesty. Human kind may not
from the earthly paths travel up there   735
in the flesh with the bright company,
the messengers of glory. You created them
and made them your attendants,
holy and heavenly. Of those in rank six are
named in eternal joy,   740
who are also surrounded and adorned
with six wings, shining brightly.
Of those there are four who, in perpetual flight,
observe in glory the service
before the face of the eternal judge,   745
continuously sing in glory
with clear voices the praise of the king of heaven,
the most beautiful of songs and utter these words
with pure voices — they are called the cherubim:
'Holy is the holy God of the archangels,   750
the ruler of hosts. Heaven and earth
are full of his wonder, and all his sublime power is shown
forth in glory.' There are two of them,
of the victory race in the sky, who are called
by the name of seraphim. He must keep   755
paradise and the tree of life holy with
a flaming sword. The hard edge quakes,
the patterned sword quivers, and the color changes,
terrible in his grip. You, Lord God,

760 wealdest widan fyrhð,   ond þu womfulle
scyld-wyrcende   sceaðan of radorum
awurpe won-hydige.   Þa sio werge sceolu
under heolstor-hofu   hreosan sceolde
in wita forwyrd,   þær hie in wylme nu
765 dreogaþ deað-cwale   in dracan fæðme,
þeostrum forþylmed.   He þinum wiðsoc
aldordome.   Þæs he in ermðum sceal,
ealra fula ful,   fah þrowian,
þeow-ned þolian.   Þær he þin ne mæg
770 word aweorpan,   is in witum fæst,
ealre synne fruma,   susle gebunden.
Gif þin willa sie,   wealdend engla,
þæt ricsie   se ðe on rode wæs,
ond þurh Marian   in middan-geard
775 acenned wearð   in cildes had,
þeoden engla,   —gif he þin nære
sunu synna leas,   næfre he soðra swa feala
in woruld-rice   wundra gefremede
dogor-gerimum;   no ðu of deaðe hine
780 swa þrymlice,   þeoda wealdend,
aweahte for weorodum,   gif he in wuldre þin
þurh ða beorhtan   bearn ne wære—
gedo nu, Fæder engla,   forð beacen þin.
Swa ðu gehyrdest   þone halgan wer
785 Moyses on meðle,   þa ðu, mihta God,
geywdest þam eorle   on þa æðelan tid
under beorh-hliðe   ban Iosephes,
swa ic þe, weroda wyn,   gif hit sie willa þin,
þurg þæt beorhte gesceap   biddan wille

will rule this for ever, and you will cast down the 760
sinful, guilty, foolish wretches
from the firmament. Then the cursed band
had to fall into the dark habitations,
into a perdition of torments, where in surging fire they
now endure death-agony in the dragon's embrace, 765
enveloped in darkness. He renounced your
authority. For that in miseries,
full of all foulness, guilty, he must suffer,
endure bondage. There he may not
cast down your word; fast among torments, 770
the lord of all sins is bound with torture.
If it be your will, ruler of angels,
that he, prince of angels, who was on the cross
should rule and through Mary in middle-earth
be born in the form of a child 775
— if he were not your son without sins,
he never would have performed
in the worldly kingdom so many true wonders
in his number of days; nor would you, ruler of nations,
so mightily have awakened him from the dead 780
before the troops if he in glory
were not your son through the bright one —
send forth your sign now, Father of angels.
As you listened to the holy man
Moses in council when you, God of powers, 785
revealed the bones of Joseph to the man
in that noble time under the mountain slope,
so, joy of hosts, if it be your will,
through that bright creation, I want to ask

790 þæt me þæt gold-hord,   gasta scyppend,
geopenie,   þæt yldum wæs
lange behyded.   Forlæt nu, lifes fruma,
of ðam wang-stede   wynsumne up
under radores ryne   rec astigan
795 lyft-lacende.   Ic gelyfe þe sel
ond þy fæstlicor   ferhð staðelige,
hyht untweondne,   on þone ahangnan Crist,
þæt he sie soðlice   sawla nergend,
ece ælmihtig,   Israhela cining,
800 walde widan ferhð   wuldres on heofenum,
a butan ende   ecra gestealda."

X

Ða of ðære stowe   steam up aras
swylce rec under radorum.   Þær aræred wearð
beornes breost-sefa.   He mid bæm handum,
805 eadig ond æ-gleaw,   upweard plegade.
Iudas maþelode,   gleaw in geþance:
"Nu ic þurh soð hafu   seolf gecnawen
on heardum hige   þæt ðu hælend eart
middan-geardes.   Sie ðe, mægena God,
810 þrym-sittendum   þanc butan ende,
þæs ðu me swa meðum   ond swa man-weorcum
þurh þin wuldor inwrige   wyrda geryno.
Nu ic þe, Bearn Godes,   biddan wille,
weoroda will-gifa,   nu ic wat þæt ðu eart
815 gecyðed ond acenned   allra cyninga þrym,
þæt ðu ma ne sie   minra gylta,
þara þe ic gefremede   nalles feam siðum,
metud, gemyndig.   Læt mec, mihta God,

you, creator of souls, to reveal to me that   790
gold hoard that was concealed
from people for a long time. Originator of life, let
smoke rise now joyful from that place on the plain
under the orbit of the firmament,
playing in the air. I will believe the better   795
and the more firmly fix my heart,
unwavering hope, on the crucified Christ,
that he is truly the savior of souls,
eternal, almighty, the king of Israel,
ruling forever the eternal dwellings   800
of glory in the heavens without end."

                                                         x

Then from that place steam arose
like smoke under the firmament. There
the mind of the man was elated. With both hands,
blessed and skilled in law, he clapped upward.   805
Judas, wise in thought, made a speech:
"Now through truth I myself have known
in my hard thought that you are the savior
of middle-earth. Let there be ceaseless thanks to you,
God of powers, enthroned in glory, because you   810
through your wonder disclosed to me, so miserable
and so sinful, the hidden things of God's providence.
Now, Son of God, I want to ask you,
ruler of troops, now that I know that you are
the revealed and acknowledged glory of all kings,   815
that you, creator, no more be mindful of
my sins, those that I did,
not at all a few times. Let me, God of powers,

ELENE

on rim-tale   rices þines
820 mid haligra   hlyte wunigan
in þære beorhtan byrig,   þær is broðor min
geweorðod in wuldre,   þæs he wære wið þec,
Stephanus, heold,   þeah he stan-greopum
worpod wære.   He hafað wigges lean,
825 blæd butan blinne.   Sint in bocum his
wundor þa he worhte   on gewritum cyðed."
Ongan þa wil-fægen   æfter þam wuldres treo,
elnes an-hydig,   eorðan delfan
under turf-hagan,   þæt he on twentigum
830 fot-mælum feor   funde behelede,
under neolum niðer   næsse gehydde
in þeostor-cofan.   He ðær þreo mette
in þam reonian hofe   roda ætsomne,
greote begrauene,   swa hio gear-dagum
835 arleasra sceolu   eorðan beþeahton,
Iudea cynn.   Hie wið Godes Bearne
nið ahofun,   swa hie no sceoldon,
þær hie leahtra fruman   larum ne hyrdon.
Þa wæs mod-gemynd   myclum geblissod,
840 hige onhyrded,   þurh þæt halige treo,
inbryrded breost-sefa,   syððan beacen geseh,
halig under hrusan.   He mid handum befeng
wuldres wyn-beam,   ond mid weorode ahof
of fold-græfe.   Feðe-gestas
845 eodon, æðelingas,   in on þa ceastre.
Asetton þa on gesyhðe   sige-beamas þrie
eorlas an-hydige   fore Elenan cneo,

dwell among the number of your kingdom
with a portion of the holy ones   820
in the bright city, where my brother is
honored in glory, because he, Stephen,
held the covenant with you even though he
was stoned. He has the reward of battle,
prosperity without end. In books, the wonders   825
that he performed are then made known in writings."
Joyful then, single-minded in courage,
he began to delve in the earth under the sod
for the tree of glory until at a twenty-foot
depth, he found it buried   830
deep down under, hidden in the abyss
in the dark chamber. There in that sorrowful
house he came upon three crosses together,
buried in the dirt, just as
the impious ones, the race of the Jews,   835
had covered them with earth. They raised up enmity
against the Son of God, as they should not have done,
had they not obeyed the teaching of the originator
of sins. Then his mind was greatly gladdened,
his heart strengthened, his spirit inspired   840
through that holy tree after he saw that sign,
holy under the ground. With his hands, he seized
the tree of joy of glory and with the multitude raised it
from its earthen grave. The traveling warriors,
the nobles, walked into the city.   845
The single-minded, proud noblemen then placed
three victory trees before the knee of

collen-ferhðe.   Cwen weorces gefeah
on ferhð-sefan,   ond þa frignan ongan
850 on hwylcum þara beama   Bearn wealdendes,
hæleða hyht-gifa,   hangen wære:
"Hwæt, we þæt hyrdon   þurh halige bec
tacnum cyðan,   þæt twegen mid him
geþrowedon,   ond he wæs þridda sylf
855 on rode treo.   Rodor eal geswearc
on þa sliðan tid.   Saga, gif ðu cunne,
on hwylcre þyssa þreora   þeoden engla
geþrowode,   þrymmes hyrde."
Ne meahte hire Iudas,   ne ful gere wiste,
860 sweotole gecyþan   be ðam sige-beame,
on hwylcre se hælend   ahafen wære,
Sige-Bearn Godes,   ær he asettan heht
on þone middel   þære mæran byrig
beamas mid bearhtme,   ond gebidan þær
865 oððæt him gecyðde   cyning ælmihtig
wundor for weorodum   be ðam wuldres treo.
Gesæton sige-rofe,   sang ahofon,
ræd-þeahtende,   ymb þa roda þreo
oð þa nigoðan tid,   hæfdon neowne gefean
870 mærðum gemeted.   Þa þær menigo cwom,
folc unlytel,   ond gefærenne man
brohton on bære   beorna þreate
on neaweste,   —wæs þa nigoðe tid—
gingne gastleasne.   Þa ðær Iudas wæs
875 on mod-sefan   miclum geblissod.
Heht þa asettan   sawlleasne,
life belidenes   lic on eorðan,
unlifgendes,   ond up ahof

Elene in her view. The queen rejoiced in her heart
in the work and then began to ask
on which of the trees the Son of the ruler,   850
the giver of hope to men, had been hanged:
"Listen, we have clearly heard told
through holy books that two suffered
with him, and he himself was the third
on the rood tree. The heavens all grew dark   855
during that cruel time. Tell me, if you know,
on which of these three the prince of angels
suffered, the guardian of glory."
Judas, who did not fully know with certainty,
could not clearly reveal to her the victory tree,   860
on which of them the savior was raised up,
the victorious Son of God, before he commanded that
they set the trees in the middle of the famous city
among the tumult and wait there
until the almighty king revealed to them   865
a miracle before the host about the tree of glory.
The triumphant, deliberating ones sat,
raised up song around the three rood trees
until the ninth hour; they had gloriously found
a new joy. Then a multitude came,   870
not a little folk, and brought a man
borne on a bier by a company of men
very close at hand—it was the ninth hour—
a youth bereft of his soul. Then Judas was
greatly blessed in his heart there.   875
He commanded them to set down the soulless one,
the body of the unliving one deprived of life
on the ground, and he,

rihtes wemend   þara roda twa
880 fyrhð-gleaw on fæðme   ofer þæt fæge hus,
deop-hycgende.   Hit wæs dead swa ær,
lic legere fæst.   Leomu colodon
þrea-nedum beþeaht.   Þa sio þridde wæs
ahafen halig.   Hra wæs on anbide
885 oð ðæt him uppan   æðelinges wæs
rod aræred,   rodor-cyninges beam,
sige-beacen soð.   He sona aras
gaste gegearwod,   geador bu samod
lic ond sawl.   Þær wæs lof hafen
890 fæger mid þy folce.   Fæder weorðodon,
ond þone soðan   Sunu wealdendes
wordum heredon: "Sie him wuldor ond þanc
a butan ende   eallra gesceafta."

XI

Ða wæs þam folce   on ferhð-sefan,
895 in-gemynde,   swa him a scyle,
wundor þa þe worhte   weoroda Dryhten
to feorhnere   fira cynne,
lifes lattiow.   Þa þær lige-synnig
on lyft astah   lacende feond.
900 Ongan þa hleoðrian   helle-deofol,
eatol æclæca,   yfela gemyndig:
"Hwæt is þis, la, manna,   þe minne eft
þurh fyrn-geflit   folgaþ wyrdeð,
iceð ealdne nið,   æhta strudeð?
905 Þis is singal sacu.   Sawla ne moton
man-fremmende   in minum leng
æhtum wunigan.   Nu cwom el-þeodig,
þone ic ær on firenum   fæstne talde,

the revealer of right, thinking deeply,
raised up two of the crosses wise in his embrace   880
over that fated house. It stayed as dead as it was before,
the body fast on the bed. The limbs grew cold,
covered with afflictions. Then the third one, holy,
was lifted up. The corpse was waiting
until above it the cross of the prince,   885
the tree of the heavenly king,
the true sign of victory, was raised. He got up at once,
infused with spirit, his body and soul
both together. Praise was elevated there,
fair among the people. They honored the Father   890
and extolled the true Son of the ruler
with words: "Glory and thanks
of all creatures be to him without end."

XI

Then in the heart of that people,
in remembrance, as it always must be for them,   895
was a miracle that the Lord of hosts, the leader of life,
performed for the salvation of
the human race. Then there the deceitful
enemy rose up, flying in the air.
The hell-devil, the horrible adversary,   900
began crying out, mindful of evils:
"Oh, what man is this who again
through ancient strife destroys my retinue,
increases the old enmity, robs my possessions?
This is perpetual strife. Sinful souls can   905
no longer remain in my
possession. Now a stranger has come,
one whom I earlier supposed bound fast in sins,

hafað mec bereafod   rihta gehwylces,
910   feoh-gestreona.   Nis ðæt fæger sið.
Feala me se Hælend   hearma gefremede,
niða nearolicra,   se ðe in Nazareð
afeded wæs.   Syððan furþum weox
of cildhade,   symle cirde to him
915   æhte mine.   Ne mot ænige nu
rihte spowan.   Is his rice brad
ofer middan-geard.   Min is geswiðrod
ræd under roderum.   Ic þa rode ne þearf
hleahtre herigean.   Hwæt, se Hælend me
920   in þam engan ham   oft getynde,
geomrum to sorge.   Ic þurh Iudas ær
hyhtful gewearð,   ond nu gehyned eom,
goda geasne,   þurh Iudas eft,
fah ond freondleas.   Gen ic findan can
925   þurh wroht-stafas   wiðer-cyr wið ðan
of ðam wearh-treafum;   ic awecce wið ðe
oðerne cyning,   se ehteð þin,
ond he forlæteð   lare þine
ond man-þeawum   minum folgaþ,
930   ond þec þonne sendeð   in þa sweartestan
ond þa wyrrestan   wite-brogan,
þæt ðu, sarum forsoht,   wiðsæcest fæste
þone ahangnan cyning,   þam ðu hyrdest ær."
Him ða gleaw-hydig   Iudas oncwæð,
935   hæleð hilde-deor,   —him wæs Halig Gæst
befolen fæste,   fyr-hat lufu,
weallende gewitt   þurh wigan snyttro—
ond þæt word gecwæð,   wisdomes ful:
"Ne þearft ðu swa swiðe,   synna gemyndig,

and has bereft me of each of rights,
of treasures. That is not a pleasant experience.   910
The Lord has done me many harms,
grievous enmities, he who was raised
in Nazareth. As soon as he grew
from childhood, he always turned
my possessions to himself. Now I cannot succeed   915
in any right. His kingdom is broad
across middle-earth. Mine is diminished,
my counsel under the firmament. I have no need
to praise that cross with exultation. Yes, the Lord often
enclosed me in that narrow home   920
as a sorrow to the mournful ones. Through Judas earlier
I became hopeful but now am humbled,
lacking goods, guilty and friendless,
by Judas again. But through calumnies
from hell I can find a reversal   925
against that; I will raise up another king
against you, one who will persecute your followers,
and he will despise your teaching
and will follow my sinful ways
and will send you then into the blackest   930
and the worst of terrible punishments,
so that you, afflicted with pains, will firmly renounce
the crucified king, whom you obeyed before."
Then to him the wise-minded Judas,
the man bold in battle—in him the Holy Spirit   935
was firmly planted, a fire-hot love,
fervent wit through the wisdom of the holy One—
spoke and said these words, full of wisdom:
"You do not need so quickly, mindful of sins,

940   sar niwigan   ond sæce ræran,
    morðres man-frea,   þæt þe se mihtiga cyning
    in neolnesse   nyðer bescufeð,
    syn-wyrcende,   in susla grund
    domes leasne,   se ðe deadra feala
945   worde awehte.   Wite ðu þe gearwor
    þæt ðu unsnyttrum   anforlete
    leohta beorhtost   ond lufan dryhtnes,
    þone fægran gefean,   ond on fyr-bæðe
    suslum beþrungen   syððan wunodest,
950   ade onæled,   ond þær awa scealt,
    wiðer-hycgende,   wergðu dreogan,
    yrmðu butan ende."   Elene gehyrde
    hu se feond ond se freond   geflitu rærdon,
    tir-eadig ond trag,   on twa halfa,
955   synnig ond gesælig.   Sefa wæs þe glædra
    þæs þe heo gehyrde   þone helle-sceaþan
    oferswiðedne,   synna bryttan,
    ond þa wundrade   ymb þæs weres snyttro,
    hu he swa geleafful   on swa lytlum fæce
960   ond swa uncyðig   æfre wurde,
    gleawnesse þurhgoten.   Gode þancode,
    wuldor-cyninge,   þæs hire se willa gelamp
    þurh Bearn Godes   bega gehwæðres,
    ge æt þære gesyhðe   þæs sige-beames,
965   ge ðæs geleafan   þe hio swa leohte oncneow,
    wuldorfæste gife   in þæs weres breostum.

XII

    Ða wæs gefrege   in þære folc-sceare,
    geond þa wer-þeode   wide læded,
    mære morgen-spel   manigum on andan

to renew the pain and raise strife,   940
wicked ruler of crime, so that the mighty king
will hurl you down into the abyss,
sinful, into the chasm of tortures
lacking renown, he who awoke many dead
with his word. May you know more clearly   945
that you unwisely have lost
the brightest of lights and the love of the Lord,
that fair delight, and on a bath of fire
encompassed with tortures have since dwelled,
burning on the pyre, and there always must,   950
malevolent, suffer damnation,
miseries without end." Elene heard
how the fiend and the friend raised debate,
the glorious and the evil, on both sides,
the sinful and the blessed. Her heart was the gladder   955
because she heard the hell-wretch
overcome, the giver of sins,
and then marveled at the wisdom of the man,
how he, so ignorant, could ever become
so full of faith in so little time,   960
suffused with prudence. She thanked God,
the king of glory, because her desire in
two things had been realized through the Son of God,
both at the sight of the victory tree,
and in the faith that she so clearly recognized,   965
the glorious gift in the man's breast.

XII

Then, to the vexation of many
of those who wanted to hide the law of the Lord,
the glorious morning news was reported

970 þara þe Dryhtnes æ   dyrnan woldon,
boden æfter burgum,   swa brimo fæðmeð,
in ceastra gehwære,   þæt Cristes rod,
fyrn foldan begræfen,   funden wære,
selest sige-beacna   þara þe sið oððe ær
975 halig under heofenum   ahafen wurde,
ond wæs Iudeum   gnorn-sorga mæst,
werum wan-sæligum,   wyrda laðost,
þær hie hit for worulde   wendan meahton,
cristenra gefean.   Ða sio cwen bebead
980 ofer eorl-mægen   aras fysan
ricene to rade.   Sceoldon Rom-warena
ofer heanne holm   hlaford secean
ond þam wiggende   wil-spella mæst
seolfum gesecgan,   þæt ðæt sigor-beacen
985 þurh meotodes est   meted wære,
funden in foldan,   þæt ær feala mæla
behyded wæs   halgum to teonan,
cristenum folce.   Þa ðam cininge wearð
þurh þa mæran word   mod geblissod,
990 ferhð gefeonde.   Næs þa fricgendra
under gold-homan   gad in burgum,
feorran geferede.   Wæs him frofra mæst
geworden in worlde   æt ðam will-spelle,
hlihende hyge,   þe him here-ræswan
995 ofer east-wegas,   aras brohton,
hu gesundne sið   ofer swon-rade
secgas mid sige-cwen   aseted hæfdon

in that nation widely among the people,   970
announced through the towns, which the sea encircles,
in every city, that the cross of Christ,
once buried in the earth, had been found,
the best of victory trees of those
holy under the heavens that had ever been raised,   975
and to the Jews, to the unhappy men, it was
the greatest of sorrows, the most loathsome of fates,
since they could not for the world change it, the joy
of the Christians. Then throughout her host of men
the queen ordered messengers to hasten   980
quickly on a journey. They had to seek
the lord of the Romans across the high sea
and to tell the warrior themselves the greatest of
joyful news, that that victory tree
had been discovered by the grace of the creator,   985
had been found in the earth, which had been hidden
before for many a season as a grief to the holy,
to the Christian folk. Then the king's mind
became gladdened by the glorious words,
his heart joyful. There was no lack of inquirers   990
in garments ornamented with gold in the cities,
traveling from afar. The greatest of consolations
in the world was created for them by the joyful news,
a rejoicing spirit, which to them the leaders,
the messengers brought over the eastern paths,   995
how safe a journey over the swan's road
the men with the victory queen had made

on Creca land.   Hie se casere heht
ofstum myclum   eft gearwian
1000   sylfe to siðe.   Secgas ne gældon
syððan andsware   edre gehyrdon,
æðelinges word.   Heht he Elenan hæl
abeodan beadu-rofre,   gif hie brim nesen
ond gesundne sið   settan mosten,
1005   hæleð hwæt-mode,   to þære halgan byrig.
Heht hire þa aras   eac gebeodan
Constantinus   þæt hio cirican þær
on þam beorh-hliðe   begra rædum
getimbrede,   tempel Dryhtnes
1010   on Caluarie   Criste to willan,
hæleðum to helpe,   þær sio halige rod
gemeted wæs,   mærost beama
þara þe gefrugnen   fold-buende
on eorð-wege.   Hio geefnde swa,
1015   siððan wine-magas   westan brohton
ofer lagu-fæsten   leof-spell manig.
Ða seo cwen bebead   cræftum getyde
sundor asecean   þa selestan,
þa þe wrætlicost   wyrcan cuðon
1020   stan-gefogum,   on þam stede-wange
girwan Godes tempel,   swa hire gasta weard
reord of roderum.   Heo þa rode heht
golde beweorcean   ond gim-cynnum,
mid þam æðelestum   eorcnan-stanum

into the land of the Greeks. The emperor commanded
them to prepare with great haste
for a return journey. The men did not hesitate   1000
once they heard his response, the word
of the prince. He commanded those renowned in war
to offer greeting to Elene, if they, the bold men,
could survive the sea and achieve
a safe journey to the holy city.   1005
Constantine also commanded the messengers to ask
her to build a church there
on the mountain slope for the good fortune
of both of them, a temple of the Lord
on Calvary as a joy to Christ,   1010
as a help for men, there where the holy rood
was found, the most famous of trees
of those that earth-dwellers have heard about
on the earthly path. She did so,
after her kinsmen brought from the west   1015
many glad tidings over the fastness of the water.
Then the queen ordered the
men taught best in their craft to be sought individually,
those who knew how to work most wondrously
in the mason's arts, to build on that place   1020
the temple of God, as the guardian of souls had guided
her from the firmament. She then commanded
that the rood be adorned with gold and gemstones,
cunningly studded with the noblest jewels

1025   besettan searo-cræftum   ond þa in seolfren fæt
       locum belucan.   Þær þæt lifes treo,
       selest sige-beama,   siððan wunode
       æðelum anbręce.   Þær bið a gearu
       wraðu wann-halum   wita gehwylces,
1030   sæce ond sorge.   Hie sona þær
       þurh þa halgan gesceaft   helpe findaþ,
       godcunde gife.   Swylce Iudas onfeng
       æfter fyrst-mearce   fulwihtes bæð,
       ond geclænsod wearð   Criste getrywe,
1035   lif-wearde leof.   His geleafa wearð
       fæst on ferhðe,   siððan frofre Gast
       wic gewunode   in þæs weres breostum,
       bylde to bote.   He þæt betere geceas,
       wuldres wynne,   ond þam wyrsan wiðsoc,
1040   deoful-gildum,   ond gedwolan fylde,
       unrihte æ.   Him wearð ece rex,
       meotud milde, God,   mihta wealdend.

XIII
       Þa wæs gefulwad   se ðe ær feala tida
       gelæded wæs   in þæt leoht gearu . . .
1045   inbryrded breost-sefa   on þæt betere lif,
       gewended to wuldre.   Huru, wyrd gescreaf
       þæt he swa geleaffull   ond swa leof Gode
       in world-rice   weorðan sceolde,
       Criste gecweme.   Þæt gecyðed wearð,
1050   siððan Elene heht   Eusebium
       on ræd-geþeaht,   Rome bisceop,
       gefetian on fultum,   forð-snoterne,

and then shut up in a silver chest   1025
with locks. There that tree of life,
the best of victory trees, has ever since remained,
inviolable in nature. There for the infirm will always be
ready a support for each of torments,
in strife and sorrow. They,   1030
through that holy creation there, will instantly find help,
a divine gift. Likewise Judas received
after a space of time the bath of baptism
and became cleansed by faith in Christ,
dear to the guardian of life. His belief became   1035
fixed in his heart, after the Spirit of consolation
took up abode in the man's breast,
encouraging him to repentance. He chose the better
thing, the joy of glory, and renounced the worse,
idolatries, and error laid low,   1040
wrong law. To him the eternal king,
the creator, God, the ruler of mights was gracious.

XIII

Then he was baptized, he who many times before
was brought ready into that light . . .
inspired his heart to the better life,   1045
turned to glory. Indeed, fate decreed
that he must become so full of faith
and so beloved of God in the worldly kingdom,
pleasing to Christ. That was made clear
when Elene commanded Eusebius   1050
in counsel, the bishop of Rome,
the very wise man, to be fetched for help,

hæleða gerædum   to þære halgan byrig,
þæt he gesette   on sacerdhad
1055 in Ierusalem   Iudas þam folce
to bisceope   burgum on innan,
þurh gastes gife   to Godes temple
cræftum gecorene,   ond hine Cyriacus
þurh snyttro geþeaht   syððan nemde
1060 niwan stefne.   Nama wæs gecyrred
beornes in burgum   on þæt betere forð,
"æ hælendes."   Þa gen Elenan wæs
mod gemynde   ymb þa mæran wyrd,
geneahhe for þam næglum   þe ðæs nergendes
1065 fet þurhwodon   ond his folme swa some,
mid þam on rode wæs   rodera wealdend
gefæstnod, Frea mihtig.   Be ðam frignan ongan
cristenra cwen,   Cyriacus bæd
þæt hire þa gina   gastes mihtum
1070 ymb wundor-wyrd   willan gefylde,
onwrige wuldor-gifum,   ond þæt word acwæð
to þam bisceope;   bald reordode:
"Þu me, eorla hleo,   þone æðelan beam,
rode rodera cininges   ryhte getæhtesð,
1075 on þa ahangen wæs   hæðenum folmum
gasta geocend,   Godes agen Bearn,
nerigend fira.   Mec þæra nægla gen
on fyrhð-sefan   fyrwet myngaþ.

with a retinue of men to the holy city,
so that he appointed Judas to the priesthood
in Jerusalem as bishop for the people   1055
within the city,
through the gift of the spirit chosen for his skills
to the temple of God, and afterward
through wise thought named him afresh,
Cyriacus. The man's name was changed   1060
for the better in the cities from then on to
"the law of the savior." Then the heart of Elene
still frequently remembered the glorious event
because of the nails that pierced the feet
and likewise the hands of the savior and   1065
with which the ruler of the firmament,
the Lord almighty, was fastened to the cross. The queen
of the Christians began to inquire about them, asked
    Cyriacus
by the power of the spirit that her wish about
the wondrous fate yet again be fulfilled,   1070
that by his wondrous gifts he should disclose it, and
spoke these words to the bishop; the bold one spoke:
"You, protector of men, to me have rightly revealed
the noble tree, the cross of the king of the firmament,
on which the helper of souls,   1075
God's own Son, the savior of men,
was hanged by the hands of men. Curiosity about the
nails still urges me on in my heart.

Wolde ic þæt ðu funde   þa ðe in foldan gen
1080   deope bedolfen   dierne sindon,
heolstre behyded.   A min hige sorgað;
reonig reoteð   ond geresteð no
ærþan me gefylle   Fæder ælmihtig,
wereda wealdend,   willan minne,
1085   niða nergend,   þurh þara nægla cyme,
halig of hiehða.   Nu ðu hrædlice
eallum eaðmedum,   ar selesta,
þine bene onsend   in ða beorhtan gesceaft,
on wuldres wyn.   Bide wigena þrym
1090   þæt þe gecyðe,   cyning ælmihtig,
hord under hrusan   þæt gehyded gen,
duguðum dyrne,   deogol bideð."
Þa se halga ongan   hyge staðolian,
breostum onbryrded,   bisceop þæs folces.
1095   Glæd-mod eode   gumena þreate
God hergendra,   ond þa geornlice
Cyriacus   on Caluarię
hleor onhylde,   hyge-rune ne mað,
gastes mihtum   to Gode cleopode
1100   eallum eaðmedum,   bæd him engla weard
geopenigean   uncuðe wyrd,
niwan on nearwe,   hwær he þara nægla swiðost
on þam wang-stede   wenan þorfte.
Leort ða tacen forð,   þær hie to sægon,
1105   Fæder, frofre Gast,   ðurh fyres bleo
up eðigean   þær þa æðelestan
hæleða gerædum   hydde wæron
þurh nearu-searwe,   næglas on eorðan.
Ða cwom semninga   sunnan beorhtra

I want you to find them, still in the earth
deeply buried and hidden,   1080
concealed in darkness. My mind will always grieve;
sorrowful, it will lament and will not cease
until the Father almighty,
the ruler of hosts, the savior of human beings,
the holy one from the heights fulfills my desire   1085
through the arrival of the nails. Now,
best of messengers, quickly and in all humility
send your petition into the bright creation,
into the joy of glory. Ask the glory of warriors,
the king almighty, to reveal to you   1090
the hoard under the ground that still remains hidden,
concealed from the retinues, secret."
Then the holy bishop of that people,
inspired in heart, began to make firm his mind.
Joyful he walked with a troop of men   1095
praising God, and then eagerly
on Calvary Cyriacus
bowed his head, did not conceal the secret of the heart,
and by the power of the spirit called to God
with all humility, prayed that the guardian of angels   1100
open to him the unknown fate,
new in difficulty, where he could most likely
expect those nails to be in that place.
Then the Father, the consoling Spirit, caused a sign
in the form of fire to rise up   1105
where they saw where the noblest nails
by the agency of men through cunning
were hidden in the earth.
Then suddenly brighter than the sun came

1110 lacende lig.   Leode gesawon
hira will-gifan   wundor cyðan,
ða ðær of heolstre,   swylce heofon-steorran
oððe god-gimmas,   grunde getenge,
næglas of nearwe   neoðan scinende
1115 leohte lixton.   Leode gefægon,
weorud will-hreðig,   sægdon wuldor Gode
ealle an-mode,   þeah hie ær wæron
þurh deofles spild   in gedwolan lange,
acyrred fram Criste.   Hie cwædon þus:
1120 "Nu we seolfe geseoð   sigores tacen,
soð-wundor Godes,   þeah we wiðsocun ær
mid leasingum.   Nu is in leoht cymen,
onwrigen, wyrda bigang.   Wuldor þæs age
on heannesse   heofon-rices God!"
1125 Ða wæs geblissod   se ðe to bote gehwearf
þurh Bearn Godes,   bisceop þara leoda,
niwan stefne.   He þam næglum onfeng,
egesan geaclod,   ond þære ar-wyrðan
cwene brohte.   Hæfde Ciriacus
1130 eall gefylled,   swa him seo æðele bebead,
wifes willan.   Þa wæs wopes hring,
hat heafod-wylm   ofer hleor goten,
—nalles for torne   tearas feollon
ofer wira gespon—   wuldres gefylled
1135 cwene willa.   Heo on cneow sette
leohte geleafan,   lac weorðode,
blissum hremig,   þe hire brungen wæs
gnyrna to geoce.   Gode þancode,
sigora Dryhtne,   þæs þe hio soð gecneow

a leaping fire. The people saw 1110
their ruler reveal a miracle,
when from the darkness there, like heavenly stars
or divine gems, the shining nails
from below near the bottom of the pit
shone with light. The people, 1115
the exultant host, rejoiced, said glory to God
all in unison, although they were before
through the destruction of the devil long in delusion,
turned away from Christ. They spoke thus:
"Now we ourselves see the sign of victory, 1120
the true wonder of God, although we denied it before
with lies. Now the manifest course of events
has come into the light. For this may the God
of the heavenly kingdom on high have glory!"
Then he who turned to penitence 1125
through the Son of God, the bishop of the people,
was gladdened once more. Frightened by terror,
he grabbed the nails and brought them
to the venerable queen. Cyriacus had
fulfilled all of the woman's desire, just as the noble 1130
one had asked him to do. Then there was the sound of
lamentation, hot tears poured down her face
—not at all for grief did tears fall down
over the web of filigree—the queen's desire
was fulfilled with glory. She kneeled 1135
in clear faith, exultant with bliss, and
honored the gift that had been brought to her
as a help for sins. She thanked God,
the Lord of victories, because she knew the truth

1140 ondweardlice þæt wæs oft bodod
feor ær beforan fram fruman worulde,
folcum to frofre. Heo gefylled wæs
wisdomes gife, ond þa wic beheold
halig heofonlic Gast, hreðer weardode,
1145 æðelne innoð; swa hie ælmihtig
Sige-Bearn Godes sioððan freoðode.

XIV

Ongan þa geornlice gast-gerynum
on sefan secean soðfæstnesse,
weg to wuldre. Huru, weorda God
1150 gefullæste, Fæder on roderum,
cining ælmihtig þæt seo cwen begeat
willan in worulde. Wæs se witedom
þurh fyrn-witan beforan sungen
eall æfter orde, swa hit eft gelamp
1155 ðinga gehwylces. Þeod-cwen ongan
þurh Gastes gife georne secan
nearwe geneahhe, to hwan hio þa næglas selost
ond deorlicost gedon meahte,
dugoðum to hroðer, hwæt þæs wære Dryhtnes willa.
1160 Heht ða gefetigean forð-snotterne
ricene to rune, þone þe ræd-geþeaht
þurh gleawe miht georne cuðe,
frodne on ferhðe, ond hine frignan ongan
hwæt him þæs on sefan selost þuhte
1165 to gelæstenne, ond his lare geceas
þurh þeodscipe. He hire þriste oncwæð:
"Þæt is gedafenlic þæt ðu Dryhtnes word
on hyge healde, halige rune,

now present that was often proclaimed   1140
long before from the origin of the world,
as a consolation to the people. She was filled
with the gift of wisdom, and the holy heavenly Spirit
occupied that dwelling, guarded her breast,
her noble heart; thus the almighty   1145
victorious Son of God since protected her.

XIV

She began then eagerly through spiritual mysteries
to seek piety in her heart,
the path to glory. Indeed, the God of hosts
the Father in the firmament,   1150
the almighty king, helped so that the queen got
her desire in the world. The whole prophecy had been
sung before by sages
from the beginning, just as it afterward happened
in each and every way. The queen of the people began   1155
through the gift of the Spirit eagerly and closely
and frequently to find out what use she
best and most worthily might put the nails to,
as a comfort to the retinue, what the will of the Lord
        might be.
She then ordered fetched an exceedingly wise man   1160
quickly to counsel, one who might well
through the power of wisdom have advice,
wise in heart, and began to ask him
what seemed to him best in his mind
to do about this, and through his instruction,   1165
she followed his teaching. He said boldly to her:
"That is fitting that you hold the word of the Lord,
holy secrets, in your thought,

223

cwen seleste,   ond þæs cininges bebod
1170 georne begange,   nu þe God sealde
sawle sige-sped   ond snyttro cræft,
nerigend fira.   Þu ðas næglas hat
þam æðelestan   eorð-cyninga
burg-agendra   on his bridels don,
1175 meare to midlum.   Þæt manigum sceall
geond middan-geard   mære weorðan,
þonne æt sæcce mid þy   oferswiðan mæge
feonda gehwylcne,   þonne fyrd-hwate
on twa healfe   tohtan secaþ,
1180 sweord-geniðlan,   þær hie sigor willað,
wrað wið wraðum.   He ah æt wigge sped,
sigor æt sæcce,   ond sybbe gehwær,
æt gefeohte frið,   se ðe foran lædeð
bridels on blancan,   þonne beadu-rofe
1185 æt gar-þræce,   guman gecoste,
berað bord ond ord.   Þis bið beorna gehwam
wið æglæce   unoferswiðed
wæpen æt wigge.   Be ðam se witga sang,
snottor searu-þancum,   — sefa deop gewod,
1190 wisdomes gewitt—   he þæt word gecwæð:
'Cuþ þæt gewyrðeð   þæt þæs cyninges sceal
mearh under modegum   midlum geweorðod,
bridels-hringum.   Bið þæt beacen Gode
halig nemned,   ond se hwæt-eadig,
1195 wigge weorðod,   se þæt wicg byrð.'"
Þa þæt ofstlice   eall gelæste
Elene for eorlum.   Æðelinges heht,

best of queens and that you eagerly abide by
the bidding of the king, now that God,   1170
the savior of human beings, has given victory
and the craft of wisdom to your soul. Have the noblest
of earthly kings, of princes,
put those nails on his bridle
as a bit for his horse. Throughout middle-earth,   1175
that will become famous to many,
since with this he may overcome
each of enemies in combat, when on
both sides brave swordsmen
seek battle, where they want victory,   1180
foe against foe. He will have success in war,
victory in combat, and everywhere peace,
protection in the fighting, he who carries in front
the bridle on the steed, when battle-brave
in the spear-storm, the choicest men   1185
bear shields and points. This will be to each of men
an invincible weapon against distress
in combat. About that the prophet sang,
wise in subtle thoughts — his mind went deep,
his understanding of wisdom — he spoke these words: 1190
'It will become known by the bit,
by the bridle rings, that the horse of the king
shall be honored among the brave. That sign will be
called holy to God, and that one fortunate,
honored in war, whom the horse bears.'"   1195
Then quickly Elene performed all that before her men.
She ordered a bridle adorned for the prince,

beorna beag-gifan,   bridels frætwan,
hire selfre suna   sende to lace
1200 ofer geofenes stream   gife unscynde.
Heht þa tosomne   þa heo seleste
mid Iudeum   gumena wiste,
hæleða cynnes,   to þære halgan byrig
cuman in þa ceastre.   Þa seo cwen ongan
1205 læran leofra heap   þæt hie lufan Dryhtnes,
ond sybbe swa same   sylfra betweonum,
freondræddenne,   fæste gelæston
leahtorlease   in hira lifes tid,
ond þæs latteowes   larum hyrdon,
1210 cristenum þeawum,   þe him Cyriacus
bude, boca gleaw.   Wæs se bissceophad
fægere befæsted.   Oft him feorran to
laman, lim-seoce,   lefe cwomon,
healte, heoru-dreorige,   hreofe ond blinde,
1215 heane, hyge-geomre;   symle hælo þær
æt þam bisceope,   bote fundon
ece to aldre.   Ða gen him Elene forgeaf
sinc-weorðunga,   þa hio wæs siðes fus
eft to eðle,   ond þa eallum bebead
1220 on þam gum-rice   God hergendum,
werum ond wifum,   þæt hie weorðeden
mode ond mægene   þone mæran dæg,
heortan gehigdum,   in ðam sio halige rod
gemeted wæs,   mærost beama
1225 þara þe of eorðan   up aweoxe,
geloden under leafum.   Wæs þa lencten agan
butan syx-nihtum   ær sumeres cyme

the ring-giver of men,
sent it as a gift, a noble offering,
to her own son over the ocean stream.   1200
Then she commanded
the best of men she knew among the Jews,
of the human race, to gather together in the holy fortress
in the city. Then the queen began
to teach the band of dear ones to firmly maintain   1205
the love of the Lord, and peace, friendship,
among themselves,
sinless in their lifetime,
and obey the teachings of that leader,
the Christian customs that to them Cyriacus,   1210
wise in books, offered. The bishopric was
well established. Often from afar
the lame, the maimed, the infirm came to him,
the halt, the very sorrowful, the leprous, and the blind,
the wretched, the sad at heart; always there   1215
they found health and remedy from the bishop,
for ever and ever. Then again Elene gave him
costly treasures when she was ready for the journey
back to her homeland, and then she enjoined all
those in that earthly kingdom praising God,   1220
men and women, that they should honor
with mind and strength, with the thoughts
of their hearts, that illustrious day when the holy rood
was found, the most glorious of trees
that has risen up from the earth,   1225
growing under its leaves. Spring had then progressed
to within six nights before the coming of summer

on Maias kalend.   Sie þara manna gehwam
behliden helle duru,   heofones ontyned,
1230   ece geopenad   engla rice,
dream unhwilen,   ond hira dæl scired
mid Marian,   þe on gemynd nime
þære deorestan   dæg-weorðunga
rode under roderum,   þa se ricesða
1235   ealles ofer-wealdend   earme beþeahte.

FINIT.

XV

Þus ic frod ond fus   þurh þæt fæcne hus
word-cræftum wæf   ond wundrum læs,
þragum þreodude   ond geþanc reodode
nihtes nearwe.   Nysse ic gearwe
1240   be ðære rode riht   ær me rumran geþeaht
þurh ða mæran miht   on modes þeaht
wisdom onwreah.   Ic wæs weorcum fah,
synnum asæled,   sorgum gewæled,
bitrum gebunden,   bisgum beþrungen,
1245   ær me lare onlag   þurh leohtne had
gamelum to geoce,   gife unscynde
mægen-cyning amæt   ond on gemynd begeat,
torht ontynde,   tidum gerymde,
ban-cofan onband,   breost-locan onwand,
1250   leoðu-cræft onleac.   Þæs ic lustum breac,
willum in worlde.   Ic þæs wuldres treowes
oft, nales æne,   hæfde in-gemynd
ær ic þæt wundor   onwrigen hæfde
ymb þone beorhtan beam,   swa ic on bocum fand,

in the month of May. For everyone of those
who hold in memory the festival of the most precious
rood under the firmament which the most mighty   1230
Lord covered with his arms,
may the door of hell be closed over, of heaven revealed,
the kingdom of angels eternally opened,
joy everlasting, and their part
assigned them with Mary.   1235

FINIT.

xv

Thus I, wise and ready to depart because of my old body,
have woven and wondrously gathered my word-craft,
at times have deliberated and sifted my thoughts
in the closeness of night. I did not clearly know
the truth about the cross before wisdom by its glorious   1240
power revealed to me a more spacious understanding
in the thought of my mind. I was stained by my deeds,
fettered by sins, afflicted by sorrows,
bitterly bound, encircled by afflictions,
before the mighty king gloriously bestowed on me   1245
his teaching as a comfort in my old age, meted out
the noble gift and begot it in my mind,
disclosed the brightness, extended it at times,
unbound my bone-coffer, loosened my breast-hoard,
unlocked the craft of poetry. I have used that   1250
with pleasure, with joy in the world. Often, not just once,
before I disclosed the miracle
about that bright tree,
I have had it in mind as I found it

1255 wyrda gangum, on gewritum cyðan
be ðam sige-beacne. A wæs secg oð ðæt
cnyssed cear-welmum, ᚲ drusende,
þeah he in medo-healle maðmas þege,
æplede gold. ᚻ gnornode,

1260 ᚾ, gefera, nearu-sorge dreah,
enge rune, þær him ᛗ fore
mil-paðas mæt, modig þrægde
wirum gewlenced. ᚹ is geswiðrad,
gomen æfter gearum, geogoð is gecyrred,

1265 ald onmedla. ᚢ wæs geara
geogoðhades glæm. Nu synt gear-dagas
æfter fyrst-mearce forð gewitene,
lif-wynne geliden, swa ᛚ toglideð,
flodas gefysde. ᚠ æghwam bið

1270 læne under lyfte; landes frætwe
gewitaþ under wolcnum winde geliccost,
þonne he for hæleðum hlud astigeð,
wæðeð be wolcnum, wedende færeð
ond eft semninga swige gewyrðeð,

1275 in ned-cleofan nearwe geheaðrod,
þream forþrycced; swa þeos world
eall gewiteð,
ond eac swa some þe hire on wurdon
atydrede, tion-leg nimeð,

1280 ðonne Dryhten sylf dom geseceð
engla weorude. Sceall æghwylc ðær
reord-berendra riht gehyran
dæda gehwylcra þurh þæs deman muð,
ond worda swa same wed gesyllan,

in the course of events, in books, made known in writings   1255
concerning that sign of victory. Always until that point
the man was tossed with surging cares, ᚲ sinking,
even though he received treasures, embossed
gold, in the meadhall. ᚨ grieved
ᛏ, a companion, endured affliction,   1260
a cruel mystery, where before him ᛗ
measured the milestoned roads, ran proud,
adorned with filigree. ᛈ is diminished,
and game, with the years; youth is changed,
old pomp. ᚢ was once   1265
the radiance of youth. Now the days of old,
after the appointed interval, have departed,
the joy of life gone, just as ᛚ, the hastening flood,
glides away. For everyone under the sky ᚹ is
fleeting; the adornments of the land   1270
depart under the clouds most like the wind
when it rises up loud before people,
hunts along the clouds, raging travels on
and again suddenly falls still,
narrowly confined in prison,   1275
suppressed with violence;
thus this world will completely depart,
and destroying flame will also take
those who were engendered in it,
when the Lord himself seeks judgment   1280
with his band of angels. Every speech-bearer
must hear truth there
through the judge's mouth about every deed
and for every word as well, be responsible

1285   eallra unsnyttro   ær gesprecenra,
þristra geþonca.   Þonne on þreo dæleð
in fyres feng   folc anra gehwylc,
þara þe gewurdon   on widan feore
ofer sidne grund.   Soðfæste bioð
1290   yfemest in þam ade,   eadigra gedryht,
duguð dom-georne,   swa hie adreogan magon
ond butan earfeðum   eaðe geþolian,
modigra mægen.   Him gemetgaþ eall
eldes leoma,   swa him eðost bið,
1295   sylfum geseftost.   Synfulle beoð,
mane gemengde,   in ðam midle þread,
hæleð hige-geomre,   in hatne wylm,
þrosme beþehte.   Bið se þridda dæl,
awyrgede wom-sceaðan,   in þæs wylmes grund,
1300   lease leod-hatan,   lige befæsted
þurh ær-gewyrht,   arleasra sceolu,
in gleda gripe.   Gode no syððan
of ðam morðor-hofe   in gemynd cumað,
wuldor-cyninge,   ac hie worpene beoð
1305   of ðam heaðu-wylme   in helle-grund,
torn-geniðlan.   Bið þam twam dælum
ungelice.   Moton engla Frean
geseon, sigora God.   Hie asodene beoð,
asundrod fram synnum,   swa smæte gold
1310   þæt in wylme bið   womma gehwylces
þurh ofnes fyr   eall geclænsod,
amered ond gemylted.   Swa bið þara manna ælc

for all folly spoken before, for presumptuous   1285
thoughts. Then into the embrace of the fire,
he will divide into three each people
who ever existed
across the spacious ground. The steadfast in truth,
the company of the blessed, the retinue of those   1290
eager for glory, will be uppermost on the pyre so that they,
a host of the brave, may tolerate it and without distress
easily endure. For them he will moderate
the full light of the fire as it will be most pleasant for him,
most easy to bear for them. The sinful,   1295
mingled with evil, sad men, will be tormented
in the middle in the hot, surging fire,
overwhelmed with vapors. The third part,
cursed sinners, false tyrants, through former works
will be secured by the flame at the bottom of the surging   1300
fire, a shoal of impious ones
in the grip of the fire coals. Never afterward
in that place of torment will they come into God's mind,
the king of glory, but they, his bitter foes, will be cast
from the fierce flame into   1305
the abyss of hell. It will be different for the other
two parts. They will be able to see the Lord of angels,
the God of victories. They will be purified,
separated from their sins like smelted gold
that in the surging flame is cleansed   1310
from all stain through the fire of the furnace,
refined and melted. So each person will be

233

ascyred ond asceaden   scylda gehwylcre,
deopra firena,   þurh þæs domes fyr.
1315   Moton þonne siðþan   sybbe brucan,
eces ead-welan.   Him bið engla weard
milde ond bliðe,   þæs ðe hie mana gehwylc
forsawon, synna weorc,   ond to Suna metudes
wordum cleopodon.   Forðan hie nu on wlite scinaþ
1320   englum gelice,   yrfes brucaþ
wuldor-cyninges   to widan feore.
Amen.

separated and held aloof from every guilt,
deep sins, through the fire of judgment.
After that, they may enjoy peace,   1315
eternal well-being. The guardian of angels will be
mild and blithe, because they despised each of evils,
the work of sins, and called to the Son of the creator
in words. Therefore they now shine in beauty
like angels, enjoy the heritage   1320
of the king of glory forever.
Amen.

Note on the Texts

The Old English texts of Cynewulf's poems reproduced for this volume are adapted from those found in volumes 2 (The Vercelli Book) and 3 (The Exeter Book) of the Anglo-Saxon Poetic Records (ASPR). Those volumes should be consulted for complete information about emendations, only the most important of which are mentioned here, along with emendations suggested by other editions of the poems, especially Muir's *The Exeter Anthology,* Roberts's *The Guthlac Poems,* Gradon's *Cynewulf's Elene,* and Brooks's *Andreas and the Fates of the Apostles.* Manuscript abbreviations and roman numerals are expanded silently; only emendations are noted in the Notes to the Texts.

Notes to the Texts

The reading adopted in the text is followed by the MS reading.

CHRIST II

471 lofedun: lufedun   491 lyfte: lyste   496 weardedun: wearde dum
503 heredun: heredum   519 gedryht: gedryt   527 bifongen: bifengun
539 hreðer: hreder   556 *A leaf is missing from the MS here*   590 wunað:
wunat   592 leofe: leohte   619 wæs: *not in MS*   621 of: ofer
644 mislicu: mislíc   698 lixeð: lixed   710 blæd: blæð   731 hell-
warena: hell werena   762 eglum: englum   790 ðy reþran: dyreþran
795 læded: lædað   827 beofiað: be heofiað   866 heofonum: to heo-
fonum

GUTHLAC B

867 gynn-wised: ginn wiseð   875 stowum: stopum   962 egle: engle
931 moste: *not in MS*   950 ælmihtiga: hælmihtiga   966 forswiðde:
for swiðede *with first e subpuncted*   969 gedælden: ge dæled   1040 ge-
sweðrad: ge swedrad   1061 drusendne: drusende   1078 edleana: edlea
nan   1091 in ead-welan: ingead welan *with g super- and subpunc-
ted*   1102 onwald: on weald   1135 þegn: *not in MS*   1143 hilde-scurum:
hilde-scurun   1215 æfen-tid: hæfen-tid   1248 life: lifes   1351 wyrd-
stafum: wyrd sta fun   1365 winiga: wiinga   1375 wæs: þæs   1379 dru-
sendne: *the end of the poem has been lost*

JULIANA

12 oft: of   16 bærndon: bærdon   46 Ic: in   86 gewealde: ge weald
90 yfel-þweorg: yreþweorg   91 glæd-mode: glæd mod   116 ænige:

239

ænig   128 þrea-niedlic: þrea med lic   151 gæsta: gæste   171 hyldo:
yldo   196 wiþer-hycgendre: wiþer hycgen de   218 meteð: me-
tet   271 gode: *not in MS*   cleopian: cleopianne   286 ealne: ealdne
with d *subpuncted*   288 dom-eadigre: dom-eadigra   294 bisweop: bis-
peop   313 asecgan: asengan   322 hell-warena: hell werena *with an* a *in-
serted above the line*   325 we: se   338 ne oðcyrreð: neod cyrreð
334 gemette: ge mete   340 geþoliað: *with* i *subpuncted*   348 soð-
fæstum: soðfæst *ends this line and* tum *begins the next*   354 siðum: sin-
don   371 hyreð: hyrað   400 gefæstnad: gefæsnad   401 wiðer-stell:
wiðsteall   437 hell-warena: hell werena *with an* a *inserted above the
line*   453 ne wende: ne ge wende *with* g *subpuncted*   456 ondettan: ond
dettan   467 þe: þy   468 oft: of   479 wege: weg   482 heoro-
dreorge:hyradreorge   485 ealde:eald   486 druncne:drucne   492 þa:
þeah   508 gewurdun: ge wordun   521 miclan: miclam   mine: min
533 halge: halige *with* i *subpuncted*   544 hel-warena: helwerena   545 is:
his   549 wif: wiþ   555 gewinnan: gewinna   559 *At least one folio is
missing from the MS here*   560 weorc: *not in MS*   562 weolde: wolde
577 bihlænan: bi lænan hearda: *not in MS*   586 Hæleð: æleð   599 meah-
tun: meahtum   620 forhogde: for hogd   628 Iuliana: Iulianan
630 fleam: flean   658 freme: *not in MS*   685 feoh-gestealda: feoh ge
stealde   687 -setle: sele   723 miclan: miclam

THE FATES OF THE APOSTLES

1 Hwæt: WÆT   4 wæron: woron   13 nearwe: neawe   84 ealle:
ealne   90 halgan: halga   93 gesecean: gesece   94 lætan: læt
96 fore-þances: forþances   98 standeþ: standaþ   119 gildeð: glideð

ELENE

12 Æðelinges: æðelnges   14 guð-weard: guð wearð   22 Hugas: hunas
26 sib: *not in MS*   31 burgende: burgenta   49 þonne: þone   68 hie:
he   90 geglenged: gelenged   119 heoru-grimme: heora grimme
124 sweotum: sweotolu   126 here-felda: hera felda   151 steran: ste-
nan   197 hyhta: hyht   242 fægerre: fægrre   245 swellingum: spell-
ingum   252 yð-hofu: yð liofu   254 hwonne: hwone   279 meðel-
hegende: meðel hengende   295 wuldres: wuldre   318 eowic: eow

322 georne: eorne   338 word: *not in MS*   348 wendo: weno   355 me:
þe   360 gifað: gifeð   379 fundon: funden   392 wære: wære wære
399 geare: eare   422 gnyrna: gnyrnra   423 orscyldne: scyldum
432 forleten: forleton   496 hie: he   501 wearð: *not in MS*   531 geh-
ðum: gehdu   561 witgan: witga   590 orde: ord   614 samod: *not in
MS*   629 him: he   629 hyht: *not in MS*   631 getæhte: ne tæhte ge
636 feala: feale   646 fyr mycle: fær mycel   661 hæleðum: hæleðu
668 on: *not in MS*   676 Caluarie: clauare   720 halige: halig
721 feondes: *not in MS*   743 sint: sit   786 geywdest: ge hwydest
836 cynn: *not in MS*   924 can: ne can   941 þe: *not in MS*   957 ofer-
swiðedne: ofer swiðende   971 boden: bodan   972 rod: *not in MS*
984 þæt: þe   996 swon-: spon   997 aseted: aseten   1025 besettan:
Be setton   1028 æðelum: æðelu   1044 gelæded wæs in þæt: *not in MS*
1074 cininges: cining   1127 þam næglum: þan næglan   1149 weroda:
weorda   1166 þriste: *not in MS*   1169 seleste: selest   1180 sigor: ymb
1183 foran: fonan   1236–51 *Note the assonance and rhyme in these lines*
1237 word-cræftum: word cræft   1240 rode: *not in MS*   1244 bisgum:
besgum *with an* i *inserted above the line*   1256 secg: sæcc   1294 eldes:
eðles

Notes to the Translations

CHRIST II

441   *mon se mæra,* "excellent man": Sisam, *Studies,* 11, suggests that Cynewulf directly addresses his patron here.

456   *Bethania,* "Bethany": A village on the southeast side of the Mount of Olives, about three kilometers from the center of Jerusalem. See Luke 24:50–53 and Acts of the Apostles 1:1–11 for the Ascension scene. See the commentary in Muir, *The Exeter Anthology,* vol. 2, for scriptural and other sources and analogues for the poem. The primary one is Gregory the Great's Homily 29 on the ascension, translated in Allen and Calder, *Sources and Analogues,* 79–81.

466–67   *feowertig . . . dagena rimes,* "forty of the count of days": See Acts of the Apostles 1:3.

499   *Him wæs geomor sefa, hat æt heortan,* "their spirit was sad, hot around the heart": Cf. *Elene,* ll. 627–28, and *Beowulf,* l. 49b.

529   *Hyht wæs geniwad,* "Hope was renewed": Cf. *The Dream of the Rood,* l. 149, and *Juliana,* l. 607.

537   *wopes hring,* "sound of lamentation": Cf. *Guthlac B,* l. 1339; *Elene,* l. 1131; *Andreas,* l. 1278.

556   A leaf is missing from the MS here.

558–70   The speaker here is not identified in the Old English text, but the context and Bede's hymn *On the Lord's Ascension,* another possible source for this poem, make clear that the angels are speaking. The "you" of l. 570 ("this same troop that you look upon here") most probably refers to the disciples. Christ's descending into hell (commonly called the Harrowing of Hell) during the three days between his death and resurrection to save the righteous dead is a doctrine of early Christian theology. See, for example, the Apostles' Creed and the apocryphal Gospel of Nicodemus (Zbigniew Izydorczyk, ed., *The Medieval Gospel of Nicodemus: Texts, Intertexts, and Contexts in Western Europe* [Tempe, 1997]). For a full discussion of the tradition, see Judith N. Garde, *Old English Poetry in Medieval Christian Perspective: A Doctrinal Approach* (Woodbridge, Suffolk, 1991), 113–30. The descent into hell is relevant to Christ's ascension because together they complete his mission of salvation for all mankind, including the Old Testament saints.

560   *unrihte swealg,* "unjustly swallowed": In an illustration in Bodleian Library Junius MS 11, p. 3, hell is depicted as a ravenous beast (perhaps a dragon) swallowing sinners, who tumble into its gaping jaws from above. Go to http://image.ox.ac.uk/show? collection=bodleian&manuscript=msjunius11.

573   *æfter guð-plegan,* "after war-play": Cf. *The Fates of the Apostles,* l. 22. The Anglo Saxons conceived of Christ and his disciples as powerful Germanic warriors. Cf. *The Dream of the Rood,* and see G. Ronald Murphy, S J, *The Saxon Savior: The Germanic Transformation of the Gospel in the Ninth-Century Heliand* (Oxford, 1989).

591–96   Rhyme, which is not a common feature of Old English verse, is used here to heighten the pace and rhetorical impact of the lines. Sporadically appearing in a handful of Old English poems, including *Beowulf,* rhyme is the dominant literary device in *The Riming Poem.*

617   *fæhþa mæste,* "the greatest of feuds": Cf. *Beowulf,* l. 109.

621   *Ic þec ofer eorðan geworhte,* "I made you from earth": See Genesis 3:19.

629   *monnes magu-tudre,* "the human race [or breed]": This phrase could be in apposition to either *us* or *leomum och lic-homan,* "limbs and body," and thus to Christ.

633–58   *Iob,* "Job": On the importance of Job in this poem as a type of Christ, see Bjork, "The Symbolic Use of Job."

651–53   *He wæs upp hafen engla fæðmum in his þa miclan meahta spede, heah ond halig, ofer heofona þrym,* "He was raised up in the embrace of

244

angels in the great wealth of his powers, lofty and holy, over the glory of the heavens": See Psalm 18:10.

659–91   On Cynewulf's use of the theme of God's gifts to human beings here, see Anderson, *Cynewulf*, 30–44.

704   *æ-fyllendra*, "destroyers of the law": According to the *Dictionary of Old English (DOE)* this word can also mean "fulfillers of the law." Since *seo circe*, "the church," needs no qualifier as the one and only church, I take it with the *DOE* to be qualifying *eaht-nysse*, "persecution."

712–43   The image of Christ's major achievements on earth as being leaps comes from the Song of Solomon 2:8, 17. For a full discussion, see note to ll. 273–304 of *The Ascension* in Muir, *The Exeter Anthology*, vol. 2.

713   *giedda gearo-snottor*, "very wise in poems": Cf. *Elene*, ll. 418 and 586.

797   *Þonne ᚳ cwacað*, "Then ᚳ will quake": The rune stands for the letter *c* and for *cen*, "torch." The Old English *Rune Poem* describes the torch as "known to all the living by its flame, shining and bright; most often it burns inside where princes sit at ease" (Halsall, *Rune Poem*, 87).

800–801   *þendan ᚣ ond ᚾ yþast meahtan frofre findan*, "while ᚣ and ᚾ could most easily find comfort": The first rune stands for *y* and *yr*, "bow," "yew," "sharp instrument," "horn." The *Rune Poem* says that "the bow is a pleasure and brings honour to all princes and nobles; it looks fine on a steed, is reliable on a journey, a kind of army-gear" (Halsall, *Rune Poem*, 93). The second rune stands for *n* and *nied*, "need" or "constraint" or "hardship." The *Rune Poem* says that *nied* "oppresses the heart; yet nonetheless often it is transformed for the sons of men to a source of help and salvation, if only they heed it in time" (89).

804–7   *Biþ se ᚹ scæcen eorþan frætwa. ᚾ wæs longe ᛁ-flodum bilocen, lif-wynna dæl, ᚠ on foldan*, "The ᚹ of the treasures of earth will have fled. ᚾ share of life-joys was long shut in by the ᛁ-streams, our ᚠ on earth": ᚹ stands for *w* and *wynn*, "joy." The *Rune Poem* explains that whoever experiences joy "knows little of woes, of pain or sorrow, and has for own prosperity and happiness and also the contentment belonging to fortified communities" (Halsall, *Rune Poem,* 87). ᚾ stands for *u* and *ur,* "aurochs," "our." The *Rune Poem* describes the aurochs as "courageous and [with] huge horns, a very fierce beast—it fights with its horns—a notorious moor-stalker; that is a brave creature" (87). ᛚ represents *l* and *lagu,* "water," which "seems interminable to men, if they are obliged to venture out in a tossing vessel, and the sea-billows terrify them exceedingly, and the sea-steed will not respond to the bridle" (91). ᚠ represents *f* and *feoh,* "wealth," "a benefit to all men; yet every man must share it freely, if he wishes to gain glory before the Lord" (87).

857   *ærþon we to londe geliden hæfdon,* "before we had sailed to land": Cf. *Juliana,* l. 677, and *Elene,* l. 249b.

860   *Godes gæst-sunu, ond us giefe sealde,* "the spiritual Son of God, and gave us the gift": Cf. l. 660.

863   *ealde yð-mearas, ancrum fæste,* "the old wave-mares, fast with anchors": Cf. *Elene,* l. 252.

GUTHLAC B

860–63   *Þære syn-wræce siþþan sceoldon mægð ond mæcgas morþres ongyldon, god-scyldge gyrn þurh gæst-gedal, deopra firena,* "Ever since, men and women, guilty against God, have had had to pay dearly for mortal sin, for deep wicked deeds, through the separation of the soul [from the body] in that punishment for sins": The main verb in this sentence (*ongyldon,* "pay") takes either the genitive or accusative, so its object can be one or all of *þære syn-wræce* (genitive or dative, "that punishment for sins"), *morþres* (genitive, "mortal sin"), *gyrn* (accusative, "pain"), and *deopra firena* (genitive, "deep wicked deeds"). Taking *þære syn-wræce* as a dative instead of a genitive, however, and *gyrn* as the adverb "dearly" (with Roberts, *The Guthlac Poems,* 160–61) leaves us with the double genitive object reflected in the translation.

942–44   *Wæs þam ban-cofan æfter niht-glome neah geþrungen, breost-hord on-boren,* "The bone-dwelling was closely oppressed in the gloom of

JULIANA

night, his breast-hoard weakened": "Bone-dwelling" is a kenning
or metaphor for "body," and "breast-hoard" is one for "mind."

1038   *dæg scriþende,* "the day having passed": This phrase may be in-
terpreted as an accusative absolute construction, modifying the
whole of the preceding sentence, or as an uninflected instru-
mental construction ("by means of the passing day") and modi-
fying *ende geseceð,* "will seek its end."

1104   *ða he from helle astag,* "when he ascended from hell": See note to
ll. 558–70 of *Christ II.*

1203   *Ic þec halsige,* "I beseech you": Cf. *Juliana,* l. 539, and *Elene,* l. 699.

1231   *butan þe nuða,* "except to you now": Cf. *Elene,* l. 661.

1281   *þrong niht ofer tiht,* "night forced itself over the expanse": This
phrase can be read either as here, taking the next line as a modi-
fier, or as being the first of two parallel variants.

1309   *beama beorhtast. Eal þæt beacen wæs,* "the brightest of trees. That
beacon was all": Cf. *The Dream of the Rood,* l. 6.

1339   *wopes hring,* "sound of lamentation": Cf. *Christ II,* l. 537; *Elene,* l.
1131; *Andreas,* l. 1278.

1379   The ending of the poem has been lost.

JULIANA

3   *Maximian:* Galerius Maximianus, emperor of Rome (305–311) af-
ter Diocletian. See entry in Simon Hornblower and Anthony
Spawforth, eds., *The Oxford Classical Dictionary,* 4th ed. (Oxford,
2003).

21   *Commedia,* "Nicomedia": Capital of the Roman province of
Bithynia and Diocletian's eastern capital. See entry in Horn-
blower and Spawforth, *Oxford Classical Dictionary.*

27   *hine fyrwet bræc,* "desire tormented him": Cf. *Elene,* l. 1078.

190   *Þis is ealdordom uncres gewynnes on fruman gefongen,* "Supremacy in
our struggle is seized from the start": This appears to be a mis-
construal of the Latin source, which may be translated, "Look,
this was just the beginning of the test" (Allen and Calder, *Sources
and Analogues,* 124).

203   *niþa gebæded,* "constrained by enmity": Cf. l. 462.

222–24   *Ic to dryhtne min mod staþelige, se ofer mægna gehwylc waldeð wide-ferh, wuldres agend, sigora gehwylces:* This passage may be translated either as here, "I will fix my mind upon the Lord, the ruler of glory, who always has dominion over each of hosts, each of victories," or as "I will fix my mind upon the Lord, the ruler of glory, of each of victories, who always has dominion over each of hosts."

288   *Heo þæt deofol genom . . . ,* "she grabbed that devil": A leaf of the manuscript is missing here, and the Latin acts of Juliana tell us what presumably is lost:

> She said to him, "Tell me, who are you; where do you come from and who sent you to me?" The demon replied, "Let me go and I will tell you." Blessed Juliana said, "You tell me first and then I will let you go." Then the demon began to speak, "I am the demon Belial, whom some call Jopher the Black. I have been entertained by men's wickednesses. I rejoice in murders. I love luxury. I embrace war. I destroy peace. It is I who made Adam and Eve transgress in paradise; I who made Cain kill his brother Abel; I who made all Job's fortune waste away; I who made the people of Israel worship idols in the desert; I who had the prophet Isaiah cut like wood by a saw; I who made King Nabuchodonosor set up an idol; I who had the three boys sent into the fiery furnace; I who caused Jerusalem to be burned; I who had the infants killed by Herod; I who made Judas betray the Son of God (I took possession of Judas so that he finished his life with a noose)."

> Allen and Calder, *Sources and Analogues,* 126

293   *Herode,* "Herod": Herod Antipas (4 BCE–39 CE). See entry in Hornblower and Spawforth, *Oxford Classical Dictionary.*

294   *Johannes,* "John": John the Baptist.

298   *Simon,* "Simon": Simon Magus, the Samarian sorcerer referred to in Acts of the Apostles 8:9–24, where Peter chastises him for trying to buy spiritual powers. The term "simony" thus comes from his name. See entry in F. L. Cross, ed., *The Oxford Dictio-*

nary of the Christian Church, 3rd ed. rev. by E. A. Livingstone (Oxford, 2005).

302   *Neron,* "Nero": Roman Emperor from 54 to 68, who persecuted Christians; according to tradition, Peter and Paul were both executed in Rome during his reign. See entry in Cross and Livingstone, *Oxford Dictionary of the Christian Church.*

304   *Pilatus,* "Pilate": Pontius Pilate, the governor of Judaea, who allowed Christ to be crucified.

307   *Egias,* "Ægias": A judge in Achaia who had St. Andrew executed. See note to l. 16 of *The Fates of the Apostles.*

308   *Andreas,* "Andrew": See note to l. 16 of *The Fates of the Apostles.*

539   *Ic þec halsige,* "I beseech you": Cf. *Guthlac B,* l. 1203, and *Elene,* l. 699.

542–45   On Christ's Harrowing of Hell, see note to ll. 558–70 of *Christ II.*

558   *hu him on siðe gelomp,* "what happened to him on the journey": Another leaf of the manuscript is missing here. The Latin analogue may be rendered:

> As Juliana came into the palace, her face seemed full of glory to everyone. When the prefect had looked at her, he said admiringly, "Tell me, Juliana, who taught you such things? How have you overcome torments as great as these with incantations?" Saint Juliana replied, "Listen to me, most irreverent prefect, and I will tell you. My Lord Jesus Christ taught me to worship the Father, the Son and the Holy Spirit. It was He who conquered your father, Satan, and his demons; it was He who sent His angel from His holy dwelling-place to help and comfort me. But you, wretch, do not know that eternal torments are prepared for you. You will endure unending tortures there, the devouring worm that never stops, and eternal darkness. Unhappy man, repent. For the Lord Jesus Christ is merciful and loving, and He wishes to save all men. He gives repentance for salvation and remission of sins."
>
> Then the prefect ordered an iron wheel to be brought in and pointed swords fixed on it; and he ordered the virgin to

be placed over the wheel so it would stand beween two columns with four soldiers on one side and four on the other. The soldiers drew up the wheel and had Juliana set upon it. After they had drawn it up, they spun the machine, and the noble body of Christ's virgin was split apart in all its members. Marrow came out of her bones and the whole wheel was bathed in it. Flames raged from the fire. Blessed Juliana, however, stood resolute in Christ's faith—her body broken, but her faith firm. And the angel of the Lord came down from heaven and put out the flame; and the chains were melted away by the fire.

Saint Juliana stood without pain and glorified God; she stretched her hand toward heaven and began to speak with tears and sighs, "Lord God almighty, you who alone possess immortality, Giver of life, Creator of all ages; you who extended the heavens with your hands and established the earth's foundations; you who fashioned man with your hands, Planter of paradise and Governor of the living tree of humanity; you who freed Lot from Sodom because of his hospitality; you who blessed Jacob and freed Joseph from the envy of his brothers (when he was sold into Egypt) and bestowed on him the honor of princes; you who sent your servant Moses into Egypt, saved him from Pharaoh's hand, and led your people through the Red Sea as if it were land; you who subjugated the foreign race, cast down the giant Goliath by the hands of your holy youth, David, and raised him to royal power; you who assumed flesh from the Virgin and were seen by the shepherds; you who are worshipped by angels and were adored by the Magi; you who revived the dead, gathered the apostles together, and commanded them to announce your kingdom; you who were betrayed by Judas, crucified in the flesh, buried in the earth, seen by the disciples after the Resurrection, and ascended into heaven; you who gave knowledge of yourself to all who believe, when you sent your apostles throughout the world; you who are the salvation of the dead, the way for those who err, the refuge for the weak: you are the one, the almighty and only true God; none can praise you for the wrong reason, but only for the right reason. I give thanks to you, God of all, you who have deigned to lead me, unworthy and sinful as I am, into your protection. And I beg, O Lord, that you deign to free me from this tyrant's malice so that he may be totally disgraced, along with his father, Satan. And I will always give glory to you forever and ever."

When she had said, "Amen," the tormentors of the city of Nicodemia cried out, "there is one God omnipotent, the God of the holy maiden Juliana and there is no other God but Him. Prefect, we repent that till now we have been led into error." And with one voice they all said, "We flee to you, O Lord. Let it suffice that we have erred thus far; henceforth we will believe in the God whom Juliana worships." Having been converted, they said to the ruler, "May all the pagan gods perish; may all who worship idols be struck down. Irreverent prefect, punish us so that we may expiate our sins, we who have worshipped idols till now. Light the fire. Think of your father's works. For henceforth we choose to have the Lord Jesus Christ as our Father, since we have been afflicted too long by your father, the devil." The prefect, filled with anger, reported everything to the Emperor Maximianus. The Emperor Maximianus passed sentence against them, and ordered all their heads cut off; but the prefect himself ordered everybody to be struck down by the sword at the same time, and one hundred and thirty men and women were beheaded.

The prefect ordered Saint Juliana, however, to be burnt alive. When Saint Juliana heard this, she stretched her hands toward heaven and said with tears, "O Lord God almighty, do not desert me, nor depart from me, nor banish me from your countenance; but be the one who helps me. Deliver me from this punishment and blot out my sins—those I may have committed in word or thought. O Lord, my kind and merciful God, have mercy on me so that my enemy, the tyrant Eleusius, may not say, 'Where is her God?'"

Allen and Calder, *Sources and Analogues*, 129–31

559   At least one folio is missing from the MS here.

559–63   Of these lines, Woolf notes that "the most reasonable inter-
pretation is to assume that these words are the conclusion of a
speech addressed by Juliana to Heliseus (that Cynewulf should
have replaced Juliana's prayer from the flames by a glorifica-
tion of God's ways spoken to Heliseus is not improbable), and
that the verbs refer to holy men from the Bible or church his-
tory, whose situations she might be likening to her own" (*Juli-
ana*, 48).

671   *þurh sweord-slege*, "through the thrust of a sword": Virgin martyrs
succumb to the sword after surviving other methods of execu-
tion because St. Paul, also a virgin, was dispatched by sword.

703–4   *Geomor hweorfeð* ᚲ ᚺ *ond* ᛏ, "Mournful, ᚲ, ᚺ and ᛏ will depart": On
these runes, see note to ll. 797 and 800–801 of *Christ II*.

706   ᛗ ᛈ *ond* ᚾ *acle bidað*, "ᛗ, ᛈ and ᚾ terrified await": ᛗ stands for *e* and
eoh, "horse" or "steed," "the joy of princes in noble company, the
charger proud in its hoofs, when warriors, prosperous ones on
horseback, discuss its points; and to the restless it always proves
a remedy" (Halsall, *Rune Poem*, 91). For the other two runes, see
note to ll. 804–7 of *Christ II*.

708–9   ᛚ ᚹ *beofað, seomað sorg-cearig*, "ᛚ ᚹ wretched will shake, tremble":
On these runes, see note to ll. 804–7 of *Christ II*.

THE FATES OF THE APOSTLES

2   *on seocum sefan*, "in my sick heart": Cf. *Guthlac B*, l. 1077.

3   *hu þa æðelingas ellen cyðdon*, "how the champions made their cour-
age known": Cf. *Beowulf*, l. 3.

6   *lof wide sprang*, "their glory spread widely": Cf. *Beowulf*, l. 18.

11   *Sume*, "Notable men": Brooks, *Andreas*, 119, construes this word
as a noun meaning "mighty men," as it can mean in *Beowulf*, l.
1113. C. L. Wrenn and W. F. Bolton, eds., *Beowulf with the Finnes-
burg Fragment*, revised 3rd ed. (Exeter, 1988), 276, translate the
word as "notable men."

13   *Nerones*, "Nero's": See note to l. 302 of *Juliana*.

16   *Andreas*, "Andrew": Late tradition has him crucified by order of

the ruler Ægias in the Greek city of Patras in Achaia in the year 60. For more information on Andrew and the other apostles, see the relevant entries in David Hugh Farmer, *The Oxford Dictionary of the Saints* (Oxford, 1978).

22   *æfter guð-plegan,* "after war-play": Cf. *Christ II,* l. 573, and note.

26   *þurh cneorisse,* "because of his family": John was the son of Zebedee (Matthew 4:21) and was brother to James. He, James, and Peter formed the inner circle of Christ's disciples.

35   *Iacob,* "James": James was the first disciple to be martyred. He was beheaded by Herod Agrippa I in the year 44 (Acts of the Apostles 12:2). Stephen was the first martyr, however. See note to l. 509 of *Elene.*

36–37   *ealdre gedælan, feorh wið flæsce,* "to part from life, to separate spirit from flesh": An instance of zeugma in which *gedælan* takes first a dative object *(ealdre)* and means "part from" and then an accusative object *(feorh)* and means "separate."

37   *Philipus,* "Philip": Some traditions have Philip dying of natural causes, others by crucifixion.

43   *Bartholameus,* "Bartholomew": He was thought to have been flayed alive before he was decapitated.

46   *Albano,* "Albanopolis": In eastern Armenia, close to the Caspian Sea.

57   *Gad:* On his resurrection, see chapters 22–23 of the Apocryphal Acts of Thomas in M. R. James, trans., *The Apocryphal New Testament* (Oxford, 1924; corrected printing, 1980), 373–74.

92   *langne ham,* "long-lasting home": I.e., the grave. The phrase derives from Ecclesiastes 12:5: "man goeth to his long home." See Brooks, *Andreas,* 122–23.

96–122   See Brooks, *Andreas,* 123–27, for notes on the numerous problems in deciphering and interpreting this passage, which is barely legible in the manuscript.

99   ᚹ *þær on ende standeþ,* "ᚹ stands at the end": On this rune, see note to ll. 804–7 of *Christ II.*

100–104   ᚠ *sceal gedreosan,* ᚢ *on eðle; æfter tohweorfan læne lices frætewa, efne swa* ᛚ *toglideð þonne* ᚳ *ond* ᚻ *cræftes neotað nihtes nearowe; on him* ᛬ *ligeð,* "ᚠ must pass away ᚢ in the native land; after that the transitory adornments of the body will disperse, even as the ᚱ vanishes when ᚲ and ᚻ exercise strength with labor in the night; ᛏ lies upon them": On these runes, see notes to ll. 797, 800–801, and 804–7 of *Christ II*.

ELENE

2–3   *tu hund ond þreo geteled rimes, swylce þrittig eac,* "two hundred and thirty-three" winters: According to a Syriac legend, the cross was first discovered by Protonike, the alleged wife of Emperor Claudius (41–54), and then was reburied by the Jews during the reign of Trajan (98–117). "Two hundred and thirty-three," then, refers to the number of years that had passed since that reburial. After the second burial, the cross was discovered again by Helena (Elene) in 326. See Drijvers, *Helena Augusta,* 147 and 173–74.

59–61   *ðæt he on Rom-wara rices ende ymb þæs wæteres stæð werod samnodon, mægen unrime,* "because they had gathered an army, a countless company, at the end of the kingdom of the Romans by the water's edge": I agree with Gradon, *Cynewulf's Elene,* 28, note to ll. 56–61, that the *he* in l. 59 must be plural (*hi* or *hie,* "they") and the singular form of the verb *samnodan (samnode)* in l. 60 simply a scribal error. I have emended the text accordingly, to the plural form *samnodon,* "they had gathered."

88–90   *Geseah he frætwum beorht wliti wuldres treo ofer wolcna hrof, golde geglenged—gimmas lixtan,* "He saw bright with treasures the beautiful tree of glory above the vault of the clouds, adorned with gold (the gems glistened)": Cf. the description of the cross in *The Dream of the Rood,* ll. 4–9.

151   *þryð-bord steran,* "to steer his mighty ship": We actually do not know what this phrase means. *Stenan,* "to stone," makes no sense, and attempts at emending the word have not been widely accepted. I follow Gradon here (*Cynewulf's Elene,* 33), however, who conjectures that the word may be *ste(o)ran,* "to steer," because *n* and *r* are fairly commonly confused.

181–82   *Alysde leoda bearn of locan deofla, geomre gastas,* "He released the sons of the people, the sorrowful souls, from the imprisonment of devils": A reference to Christ's "Harrowing of Hell." See note to ll. 558–70 of *Christ II*.

190   *Siluestre,* "Sylvester": Bishop of Rome 314–335 and, according to one legend, responsible for Constantine's and Elene's conversion to Christianity. See entry in Cross and Livingstone, *Oxford Dictionary of the Christian Church,* and Drijvers, *Helena Augusta,* 37.

509   *Stephanus,* "Stephen": The first martyr, ca. 35. He was stoned to death after accusing Israel of resisting the promptings of the Holy Spirit and of betraying and murdering the Just One, or Christ. See Acts of the Apostles 7:2–60.

634   *tu hund oððe ma,* "200 or more": See note to ll. 2–3, above.

661   *butan her nuða,* "except here then now": Cf. *Guthlac B,* l. 1231.

699   *Ic eow healsie,* "I beseech you": Cf. *Guthlac B,* l. 1203, and *Juliana,* l. 539.

723   *wæl-reste,* "place of rest on the battlefield": On Christ as an Anglo-Saxon warrior, see note to l. 573 of *Christ II*.

755   *he sceal,* "he must": The switch from the plural to the singular here is inexplicable.

765   *in dracan fæðme,* "in the dragon's embrace": See note to l. 560 of *Christ II*.

787   *ban Iosephes,* "the bones of Joseph": See Exodus 13:19 and Joshua 24:32. The reference here is to a Talmudic legend about the bones being first revealed to Moses through his prayers (Gradon, *Cynewulf's Elene,* 56, note to l. 787).

812   *wyrda geryno,* "the hidden things of God's providence": For the translation of this opaque phrase, see Gradon, *Cynewulf's Elene,* 57, note to l. 812.

880   *hus,* "house": This is a truncated form of kennings or metaphors such as *feorh-hus,* "life-house" or "body."

1050   *Eusebium,* "Eusebius": This may be Eusebius of Nicomedia, the bishop of Constantinople, who baptized Constantine. See Drijvers, *Helena Augusta,* 177 n. 53.

1062   *æ hælendes,* "the law of the savior": The name Cyriacus is actually the Latinized form of the Greek name *Kyriakos,* meaning simply, "of the lord."

1078   *fyrwet myngaþ,* "curiosity admonishes": Cf. *Juliana,* l. 27.

1131   *wopes hring,* "sound of lamentation": Cf. *Christ II,* l. 537; *Guthlac B,* l. 1339; *Andreas,* l. 1278.

1134   *wira gespon,* "web of filigree": Perhaps a reference to a broach.

1236–51   Of the conspicuous rhyme in these lines, Calder (*Cynewulf,* 164) notes that "Cynewulf chooses to discuss his craft within the passage where he most obviously demonstrates that art, where the surface tricks capture the attention . "

1257   ᚲ *drusende,* "ᚲ sinking": On this rune, see note to l. 797 of *Christ II.*

1259   ᚾ *gnornode,* "ᚾ grieved": On this rune, see note to ll. 800–801 of *Christ II.*

1260–62   ᛏ, *gefera, nearu-sorge dreah, enge rune, þær him* ᛗ *fore mil-paðas mæt,* "ᛏ, a companion, endured affliction, a cruel mystery, where before him ᛗ measured the milestoned roads": On the first rune, see note to ll. 800–801 of *Christ II.* On the second, see note to l. 706 of *Juliana.*

1263   ᚹ *is geswiðrad,* "ᚹ is diminished": On this rune, see note to ll. 804–7 of *Chrit II.,*

1265–66   ᚢ *wæs geara geogoðhades glæm,* "ᚢ was once the radiance of youth": On this rune, see note to ll. 804–7 of *Christ II.*

1268–70   *swa* ᛚ *toglideð, flodas gefysde.* ᚠ *æghwam bið læne under lyfte,* "just as ᛚ, the hastening flood, glides away. For everyone under the sky ᚠ is fleeting": On these runes, see note to ll. 804–7 of *Christ II.*

1261   *enge rune,* "cruel mystery": Gradon, *Cynewulf's Elene,* 73, note to l. 1261, observes that this may be a pun: "oppressive secret" and "narrow rune."

1276–81   *swa þeos world eall gewiteð, ond eac swa some þe hire on wurdon atydrede, tion-leg nimeð, ðonne dryhten sylf dom geseceð engla weorude,* "thus this world will completely depart, and destroying flame will also take those who were engendered in it, when the Lord himself seeks judgment with his band of angels": See 2 Peter 2:10–12.

1281–86　*Sceall æghwylc ðær reord-berendra riht gehyran dæda gehwylcra þurh þæs deman muð, ond worda swa same wed gesyllan, eallra unsnyttro ær gesprecenra, þristra geþonca,* "Every human being must hear truth there through the judge's mouth about every deed and must be responsible for every word as well, for all folly spoken before, for presumptuous thoughts": See Matthew 16:27 and 12:36.

Bibliography

This is a selected bibliography. For complete coverage, consult Stanley B. Greenfield and Fred C. Robinson, eds., *A Bibliography of Publications on Old English Literature to the End of 1972* (Toronto, 1980), and the subsequent bibliographies in the journals *Anglo-Saxon England* and *Old English Newsletter* (accessible online as OEN Bibliography database: www.oenewsletter.org/OENDB/index.php).

EDITIONS

Brooks, Kenneth R., ed. *Andreas and The Fates of the Apostles.* Oxford, 1961.

Colgrave, Bertram, ed. and trans. *Felix's Life of Saint Guthlac.* Cambridge, 1956.

Gradon, Pamela O. E., ed. *Cynewulf's Elene.* London, 1958; rev. ed. Exeter, 1996.

Krapp, George Philip, ed. *The Vercelli Book.* The Anglo-Saxon Poetic Records 2. New York, 1932.

Krapp, George Philip, and Elliott Van Kirk Dobbie, eds. *The Exeter Book.* The Anglo-Saxon Poetic Records 3. New York, 1936.

Muir, Bernard, ed. *The Exeter Anthology of Old English Poetry.* 2 vols. Exeter, 1994. The Exeter DVD version 2006.

Roberts, Jane, ed. *The Guthlac Poems of the Exeter Book.* Oxford, 1979.

Woolf, Rosemary, ed. *Cynewulf's Juliana.* London, 1954; rev. ed. Exeter, 1993.

ENGLISH TRANSLATIONS

Bradley, S. A. J. *Anglo-Saxon Poetry: An Anthology of Old English Poems in Prose Translations with Introduction and Headnotes.* London, 1982.

Gordon, R. K. *Anglo-Saxon Poetry.* London, 1967.

Kennedy, Charles W. *The Poems of Cynewulf, Translated into English Prose.* London, 1910; repr. New York, 1949.

SECONDARY SOURCES

Ai, Low-Soon. "Mental Cultivation in *Guthlac B.*" *Neophilologus* 81 (1997): 625–36.

Allen, Michael J. B., and Daniel G. Calder, ed. and trans. *Sources and Analogues of Old English Poetry: The Major Latin Texts in Translation.* Cambridge, 1976.

Anderson, Earl R. *Cynewulf: Structure, Style, and Theme in His Poetry.* London, 1983.

Biggs, Frederick M. "Unities in the Old English *Guthlac B.*" *Journal of English and Germanic Philology* 89 (1990): 155–65.

Bjork, Robert E., ed. *Cynewulf: Basic Readings.* New York, 1997; repr. as *The Cynewulf Reader,* New York, 2001.

———. *The Old English Verse Saints' Lives: A Study in Direct Discourse and the Iconography of Style.* Toronto, 1985.

———. "The Symbolic Use of Job in Ælfric's Homily on Job, *Christ II,* and *The Phoenix.*" In *Latin Learning and English Lore: Studies in Anglo-Saxon Literature for Michael Lapidge,* edited by Andy Orchard and Katherine O'Brien O'Keeffe, vol. 2, 315–30. Toronto, 2005.

Boren, James. "Form and Meaning in Cynewulf's *Fates of the Apostles.*" In Bjork, *Cynewulf,* 57–65.

Bredehoft, Thomas A. *Authors, Audiences, and Old English Verse.* Toronto, 2009.

Bridges, Margaret Enid. *Generic Contrast in Old English Hagiographical Poetry.* Copenhagen, 1984.

Brown, Michelle P. "Female Book-Ownership and Production in Anglo-Saxon England: The Evidence of the Ninth-Century Prayerbooks." In *Lexis and Texts in Early English: Studies Presented to Jane Roberts,* edited by Christian Kay and Louise Sylvester, 45–67. Amsterdam, 2001.

Calder, Daniel G. *Cynewulf.* Boston, 1981.

———. "*Guthlac A* and *Guthlac B:* Some Discriminations." In *Anglo-Saxon Poetry: Essays in Appreciation for John McGalliard,* edited by Lewis Nicholson and Dolores Warwick Frese, 65–80. Notre Dame, 1975.

———. "Theme and Strategy in *Guthlac B.*" *Papers on Language and Literature* 8 (1972): 227–42.

Campbell, Jackson J. "Cynewulf's Multiple Revelations." In Bjork, *Cynewulf,* 229–50.

Chase, Colin. "God's Presence through Grace as the Theme of Cynewulf's *Christ II* and the Relationship of this Theme to *Christ I* and *Christ III.*" *Anglo-Saxon England* 3 (1974): 87–101.

Cross, J. E. "Cynewulf's Traditions about the Apostles in *The Fates of the Apostles.*" In Bjork, *Cynewulf,* 79–94.

Das, S. K. *Cynewulf and the Cynewulf Canon.* Calcutta, 1942.

Dendle, Peter. "How Naked Was Juliana?" *Philological Quarterly* 83 (2004): 355–70.

Diamond, Robert E. "The Diction of the Signed Poems of Cynewulf." In Bjork, *Cynewulf,* 309–22.

Donoghue, Daniel. *Style in Old English Poetry: The Test of the Auxiliary.* New Haven, 1987.

Drijvers, Jan Willem. *Helena Augusta: The Mother of Constantine the Great and the Legend of Her Finding of the True Cross.* Leiden, 1992.

Earl, James W. "Typology and Iconographic Style in Early Medieval Hagiography." *Studies in the Literary Imagination* 8 (1975): 15–46. Repr. in *Typology and Medieval English Literature,* edited by H. Keenan, 89–120. New York, 1992.

Frantzen, Allen J. "Drama and Dialogue in Old English Poetry: The Scene of Cynewulf's *Juliana.*" *Theatre Survey* 48 (2007): 99–119.

Frese, Dolore Warwick. "The Art of Cynewulf's Runic Signatures." In Bjork, *Cynewulf,* 323–46.

Fulk, R. D. "Cynewulf: Canon, Dialect, and Date." In Bjork, *Cynewulf,* 3–21.

Hieatt, Constance B. "*The Fates of the Apostles:* Imagery, Structure, and Meaning." In Bjork, *Cynewulf,* 67–77.

Hall, Thomas N. "A Gregorian Model for Eve's *Biter Drync* in *Guthlac B.*" *Review of English Studies* 44 (1993): 157–75.

Halsall, Maureen, ed. *The Old English Rune Poem: A Critical Edition.* Toronto, 1981.

Hermann, John P. *Allegories of War: Language and Violence in Old English Poetry.* Ann Arbor, 1989.

Horner, Shari. *The Discourse of Enclosure: Representing Women in Old English Literature.* Albany, 2001.

Howe, Nicholas. *The Old English Catalogue Poems.* Copenhagen, 1985.

Irvine, Martin. "Cynewulf's Use of Psychomachia Allegory: The Latin Sources of Some 'Interpolated' Passages." In *Allegory, Myth, and Symbol,* edited by Morton W. Bloomfield, 39–62. Cambridge, Mass., 1981.

Johnson, David F. "Hagiographical Demon or Liturgical Devil? Demonology and Baptismal Imagery in Cynewulf's *Elene.*" In *Essays for Joyce Hill on Her Sixtieth Birthday,* edited by Mary Swan, 9–29. Leeds, 2006.

Klein, Stacy S. *Ruling Women: Queenship and Gender in Anglo-Saxon Literature.* Notre Dame, 2006.

Lionarons, Joyce Tally. "Cultural Syncretism and the Construction of Gender in Cynewulf's *Elene.*" *Exemplaria* 10 (1998): 51–68.

Liuzza, Roy M. "The Old English Christ and Guthlac Texts, Manuscripts and Critics." *Review of English Studies* 41 (1990): 1–11.

Lucas, Peter J. "Easter, the Death of St. Guthlac and the Liturgy for Holy Saturday in Felix's *Vita* and the Old English *Guthlac B.*" *Medium Ævum* 61 (1992): 1–16.

McCulloh, John M. "Did Cynewulf Use a Martyrology? Reconsidering the Sources of *The Fates of the Apostles.*" *Anglo-Saxon England* 29 (2000): 67–83.

Mussetter, Sally. "Type as Prophet in the Old English *Guthlac B.*" *Viator* 14 (1983): 41–58.

Niles, John D. "Cynewulf's Use of Initialisms in his Runic Signature." In his *Old English Enigmatic Poems and the Play of the Texts,* 285–306. Turnhout, 2006.

Olsen, Alexandra Hennessey. *Speech, Song, and Poetic Craft: The Artistry of the Cynewulf Canon.* New York, 1984.

Olsen, Karin. "Cynewulf's Elene: From Empress to Saint." In *Germanic Texts and Latin Models: Medieval Reconstructions,* edited by K. E. Olsen, A. Harbus, and T. Hofstra, 141–56. Leuven, 2001.

Orchard, Andy. "Both Style and Substance: The Case for Cynewulf." In *Anglo-Saxon Styles,* edited by George Hardin Brown and Catherine Karkov, 271–305. Albany, 2003.

Page, R. I. *An Introduction to Old English Runes.* 2nd ed. Woodbridge, 1999.

Pulsiano, Phillip. "The Sea of Life and the Ending of *Christ II*." In *Geard-agum* 5 (1983): 1–12.

Puskar, Jason R. "*Hwa pas fitte fegde?* Questioning Cynewulf's Claim of Authorship." *English Studies* 92 (2011): 1–19.

Rice, Robert C. "The Penitential Motif in Cynewulf's *Fates of the Apostles* and in His Epilogues." *Anglo-Saxon England* 6 (1977): 105–20.

Rosier, James L. "Death and Transfiguration in *Guthlac B*." In *Philological Essays: Studies in Old and Middle English Language and Literature in Honour of Herbert Dean Merritt,* edited by James L. Rosier, 82–92. The Hague, 1970.

Schaar, Claes. *Critical Studies in the Cynewulf Group.* Lund, 1949; repr. New York, 1967.

Sisam, Kenneth. *Studies in the History of Old English Literature.* Oxford, 1953.

Stodnick, Jacqueline A. "Cynewulf as Author: Medieval Reality or Modern Myth?" *Bulletin of the John Rylands University Library* 79 (1997): 25–39.

Index

Roman numerals refer to the page numbers of the Introduction, and Arabic numerals refer to the Old English poems and line numbers. The poems are numbered as follows: 1. *Christ II*, 2. *Guthlac B*, 3. *Juliana*, 4. *The Fates of the Apostles*, 5. *Elene*. An *n* after an Arabic numeral refers to the Notes to the Translations.